PRO TACTICS™

BASS

Catch More and Bigger Bass
Using the Pros' Tournament Secrets

PRO TACTICS™

BASS

Catch More and Bigger Bass
Using the Pros' Tournament Secrets

Karen Savik
and
David Dirks

Lyons Press is an imprint of Globe Pequot Press.
Pro Tactics is a trademark of Morris Book Publishing, LLC.

North American Fishing Club
12301 Whitewater Drive
Minnetonka, MN 55343
www.fishingclub.com

Cover photo by Bill Lindner Photography, blpstudio.com.

Text design by Peter Holm (Sterling Hill Productions) and Libby Kingsbury

ISBN 978-0-7627-7872-0

Printed in the United States of America

10 9 8 7 6 5 4 3 2

To my husband and daughters, whose patience and support have allowed me to pursue my tournament fishing dream.

—Karen Savik

This book is dedicated to my loving and patient family as well as the thousands of competitive anglers who enjoy bass fishing to such an extent that they dedicate a good portion of their lives to increasing their knowledge and then sharing it with others. It is also dedicated to the six professional bass anglers and especially their families, who do without them for most of the year: Paul Elias, Randy Howell, Jimmy Mason, Frank Scalish, Terry Scroggins, and Sam Swett.

—David Dirks

CONTENTS

ACKNOWLEDGMENTS

Many people worked hard to make this book possible, and I'd like to dedicate some space to thank them. For starters, my mom and dad raised me to appreciate and care for Mother Nature. I firmly believe that all anglers (or any outdoor user) should be responsible stewards for the environment, and I owe that sense of responsibility to my wonderful parents, Gene and Virginia Jenniges.

Next, if it hadn't been for my big brother, Steve Jenniges, who loaned me the money to enter my first tournament circuit as a pro fifteen years ago, this book probably never would have happened. It took me three years to pay him back, but I never would have become a hard-core tournament bass angler without his initial financial support. I had a short window of time to tackle this sport professionally, and had it not been for Steve, it wouldn't have happened for me.

My husband of twenty-seven years, Ken, and my daughters, Britta and Kirsten, deserve so much credit for their patience and support in understanding my passion for fishing, even though they don't necessarily share it. Their constant encouragement kept me going when the chips were down (and up), and when I'm on the road, I always know they're "taking care of business."

Thanks also to all the professional and amateur anglers who shared my boat or competed against me over the years. I've learned something from all of you, and you forced me to improve and play up to your incredible level. You've been great friends and made me a better angler. All my sponsors have made it possible through great products, equipment, and financial sponsorships to participate in the wonderful sport of tournament angling. Ranger Boats, Land O' Lakes, Evinrude, Lowrance, Abu-Garcia, Fenwick, Berkley, and MinnKota have been great sponsors to represent on the water and at shows and events across the country. The wonderful people at these companies have become friends for life!

On the publishing side, thank you to Tim Lesmeister and Rob Drieslein for their guidance and assistance in putting my thoughts and ideas to paper. And photographer Mitch Kezar deserves massive kudos for making this book so visually enticing: He snapped all the great images you see. He made me look good!

Finally, to the public reading these pages, thanks for your support. I'm living proof that anybody can make it in bass fishing and share his or her experience with others. Don't let any obstacles stand in the way of your doing the same!

—Karen Savik

This book wouldn't have been possible had it not been for the help I received from my good friend Ken Schultz. One of America's most prolific fishing writers, it was Ken who took the time to send me the info on this book project. He also provided invaluable contacts and advice that enabled me to put this book together. I am deeply indebted to Ken.

There are six anglers who contributed an average of five hours on the telephone or in person for in-depth interviews, and this book is based entirely on their personal and professional experiences on the bass tournament trail. Terry Scroggins, Frank Scalish, Jimmy Mason, Paul Elias, Sam Swett, and Randy Howell are among the best of the best. They held nothing back and freely shared their strategies and tactics with me.

Jeff Samsel from PRADCO enabled me to meet many of the pros in person for interviews, research, and anything else I needed. He gave generously and with heart.

Special thanks to Kelly Barefoot of Custom Lures Unlimited for sharing his expansive knowledge of bass lure design and providing custom lures used for photography for this book.

TJ Stallings from TTI Companies and Dave Washburn from the FLW Tour provided access to additional pro anglers and much in the way of resources for this book. Thanks also to Tommy Akin of Akin Promotions for sharing his public relations expertise with me and Scott Rauber for sharing his expertise on marketing to tour sponsors.

Last but certainly not least, a big thank-you to my editor, Bill Schneider. Through his advice and guidance, I've learned much more about the art, the craft, and the business of writing.

—David Dirks

INTRODUCTION

Could you fish bass for a living? Sure you could. Who wouldn't love being paid to do something they love? Being on the water every morning. Figuring out the day's pattern. Getting that first hit. Hearing the gears click in your fishing mind. Fine-tuning your approach to make the most of what's going on down below. Finding consistent success. Really pulling in the fish. Netting that hawg!

As a North American Fishing Club Member, you almost certainly have bass on your fishing target list, and they may even take up most of your angling efforts. Whether it's largemouths in a tiny farm pond or sprawling reservoir, or smallmouths in a natural lake or a swift stream, bass are always on the top of NAFC Members' minds. And while we're not tournament anglers, we sure like catching fish as if our lives depended on it!

That's why *BASS* is such an important book for you. Created by long-time fishing writer David Dirks and tournament bass professional Karen Savik, this volume takes you *inside* bass fishing, revealing tournament anglers' strategies and approaches, and setting you up for the same kind of intense fishing success.

See how the pros do their research and plan for success. Discover how tournament anglers prepare and practice. Gather tackle tips and tricks for everything from rods to knots. Learn tournament fishing strategies and pros' secrets that will put more bass in your boat. Get insights on using your electronics to their full potential. Find out what baits are best in what situations. Know how to adjust your approach across a wide range of water, weather and habitat conditions.

Tournament angling isn't for the weak of heart. It's for the aggressive, the confident, the adventurous . . . the angler with *knowledge*, and the ability to put that information to good use on the water. Maybe you won't be fishing any bass tournaments soon. But with *BASS* and all these pros' secrets guiding your approach, you'll be catching fish like your livelihood depended on it!

CHAPTER ONE

Meet the All-American Fish

Unlike some fish, a few of which I consider downright ugly, largemouth and smallmouth bass are muscular, handsome species. Millions of people fish bass because they're found across the United States (and beyond). Like people, they're active during the day, smart, and they have a big appetite, so—unlike those finicky finesse gamefish like walleyes or trout—you don't need a degree in angling-ology to pursue them. Did I mention they're loads of fun to catch? They tussle like spunky streetfighters, barreling toward the bottom after the hookset, leaping out of the water like few other freshwater species, then shaking their heads vigorously at boatside.

That's not to say the sport is "fishing in a barrel," so to speak. Bass have responded well to catch-and-release and better angling techniques during the past decade, too. Wherever I fish them, bass can handle respectful handling, a picture, then—with a flick of their tail—they bolt back out of sight. Bass are the all-American fish: They like a good tussle, live life

Opposite: The author with a chunky "largie." Bass are an extremely accessible species of fish in the United States for people of all ages, genders, and income levels. MITCH KEZAR, WINDIGOIMAGES.COM

a million miles an hour, and can thrive in places other creatures ignore. Must be why I like them so much!

Peruse the Florida-based International Game Fish Association's recordbook, and you'll see that many species of gamefish—saltwater, freshwater, and from other continents—share the name "bass." Striped bass and white bass also can be found in fresh water. I've fished stripers in Beaver Lake, Arkansas, and have many friends who've fished them off the East Coast. By whatever name, they're a rocking good time to fish. That's a topic for another book, however. For the purposes of these pages, I'm going to focus on the two black bass species most anglers think about when talking about bass fishing: smallmouth and largemouth.

Like their more southerly cousins, such as spotted bass, these species belong to the sunfish family (per the IGFA recordbook), which fish biologists call the Centrarchidae family. That's about as scientific as I'll get in these pages, but I think it's important to share that fact so that anglers understand that in one respect we're ultimately just pursuing big panfish. Little three-to-a-pound bluegills can put up a pretty good fight. You've seen them bend your son's or daughter's Snoopy pole a time or two, I'll wager. Well, imagine a 2- or 3-pound bluegill. Quite a tussle would ensue, right? So go figure that a 3- or 4-pound bass can put a hurt on your biceps when you're hauling him in! Understanding bass biology will help us in many ways later when we plan tactics and search locations.

Bass and Their Environment

Even through they live in a very different environment from people, smallmouth and largemouth bass alike rely on senses that are pretty understandable to those of us who breathe air. A quick Web search reveals that there's been a lot of research into fish vision, and scientists say bass indeed can see in color. (That's reassuring to those of us who purchase all those bizarre-colored lures to catch bass. Glad it's not just a big marketing ploy, right?) Thumb through a fishing catalog and you'll see lures representing all colors of the rainbow. Those colors may rarely exist naturally underwater, but they exist in my tackle box! I have no clue why such colors perform, but they do. In an effort to present heavily fished bass with new patterns, some modern fishing lures combine flash, translucent colors, and even glowing elements.

In turbid spring or river water, all fish rely more on their sense of smell or lateral line to locate prey.

My tournament schedule usually takes me to turbid lakes during the spring-runoff season or to rivers, where water clarity usually is pretty marginal. Here's where our knowledge of the bass's lateral line and other senses pays off. The lateral line is that faint exterior line of dots on the outside of virtually all fish. It helps them—almost sonarlike—to detect movement and vibration in the water. You'll hear fishing gurus at seminars or on radio broadcasts talk about the need to keep crankbaits and other lures properly tuned, and the lateral line is the big reason why. A well-tuned lure delivers more vibration and pulse to the water—vibration that fish will detect (and, we hope, pursue) thanks to sensing it via that lateral line. Make sense? (No pun intended.)

In these more turbid areas, where bass use their vision less to find and strike my lures, I can work the scent and noise factor to my advantage, too. You'd better believe I have rattle presentations ready for such conditions. Also regarding the noise factor, any self-respecting angler can tell you that noise scares any fish species, so I always make a conscious effort to remain as quiet as possible. People have been trying to entice fish via their sense of smell for thousands of years, and so-called high-tech, modern bass anglers are no different. My fishing experience has taught me to take the smell factor seriously, and in a tournament situation, I'll try anything that might give me an edge. Even if scented products like salt-impregnated or garlic-scented lures help enliven my bass fishing just a smidge, it's worth a shot! Also, I keep my hands as clean as possible and avoid any unnatural scent or human odors that might alarm the fish.

Locating Bass

Part of the appeal of bass and bass fishing is that these fish can inhabit so many regions and types of waters. Contacting state natural resource agencies is the quickest way to determine if a body of water near you contains largemouth or smallmouth bass. Many agencies provide lake

profile data with contour maps on their Web sites where you can quickly search which species are present. Private businesses also sell lake maps that delineate clear structure, GPS coordinates, and other data that can help streamline your search. The ability to research a lake or river thoroughly before even hitching up your boat and trailer has advanced light years since I began tournament fishing. If you enjoy traveling to new destinations to catch bass, there's no better—or easier—time than the present, thanks to the volumes of information quickly and affordably available in the digital age via software and the Internet.

If you want to search specific lakes or rivers, it's easy. But in this section, I'd like to break down some basic trends that hold for bass locations across the northern tier of the United States. Let's start with the simple lake. I'm no geologist, but a little research explains the history behind the abundance of water in the Upper Midwest, Northeast, and southern Canada. The last ice age ended 10,000 years ago, and the massive sheets of ice that covered the northern United States left all sorts of geological features scattered across the landscape. States like Wisconsin celebrate this geological past with state parks and trails dedicated to the moraines, drumlins, and coulees that remained after the ice receded. We're more interested in the large depressions those heavy glaciers carved into the ground, then filled with melted ice when the glaciers receded.

From the western Great Lakes to the Finger Lakes region of New York, the glaciers gouged out holes in the landscape. Even the hard granite of the Canadian Shield was no match for mile-thick ice, I'm told. We can thank the big blocks of ice for all those lakes that provide some of the continent's best fishing opportunities for cold-water species like walleyes, lake trout, and big northern pike. Fly over the waterworld of southern Canada, especially Ontario and Quebec, on a hunting or fishing trip, and the land looks like a creative afterthought—simple blobs of green amidst the blue lakescape.

Areas south of or between lobes of the glaciers created "driftless areas" where you won't find lakes. But the fact that glaciers didn't flatten this landscape means water has had time to erode the land and create hilly bluff country with cool meandering streams and rivers in between. Today many of those waterways contain excellent, underfished bassin' opportunities.

To this day, on my tournament circuit I'll still pursue smallmouth as far south as Arkansas, although many of my southern comrades admit

Opposite: Adult bass spend much of their life in ambush mode, waiting for unsuspecting food sources to stumble nearby and offer an easy meal. Bouncing a grub or artificial lure past or through shady structure can elicit strikes from largemouths on even the warmest, brightest days of the year. MITCH KEZAR, WINDIGOIMAGES.COM

that one reason they enjoy fishing northern tournaments is for the much greater opportunity to fish the hard-fighting, surface-busting smallmouth. Like largemouth, smallies have been stocked all over the place, but they demand cleaner, colder water than their greenish cousins.

Classic stocked smallmouth water includes much of the canoe country wilderness waterways of the Boundary Waters and Quetico region of northern Minnesota and northwest Ontario, the Adirondacks region of New York, and many points in between and elsewhere. But both species also are present in many lakes and riverways that you can access by boat, so let's break down where these fish are hiding.

Temperature-wise, largemouth are simply more tolerant of warmer water. The warmest water that ever produced largemouth for me was in the upper 80s, but most of my summertime, northern U.S. fish are in low 80-degree water. Down South they survive in waterways with summer temperatures into the high 80s. Unless it's in a large deepwater lake where they can find relief from warmer temps, most smallmouth I see prefer waterways that top out around 70 degrees. For that reason, you're rarely going to find a massive smallie in a farm pond or shallow, farm-country lake, and you're less likely to catch largemouth in a cold Canadian Shield lake. Like most American sportfish, both species require clean water, though the largemouth can survive or even thrive in less pristine waterways than the smallmouth. Given that those conditions persist across most of the Lower 48, it's no wonder that largemouth are the dominant bass species.

Even in these relatively warm lakes and reservoirs, largemouth bass seek cover for shade and to remain hidden prior to striking their prey. Vegetation, rocky outcroppings, docks, bridges, swimming platforms, or other structure offer obvious locations where you'll find bass. By the way, there's a fine line between too many weeds and not enough. A quality lake usually contains enough weeds for big bass to hide and hammer the small panfish. Too many weeds, however, prevent the bass from successfully preying on the sunnies, which can then destroy bass nests. It's a phenomenon we see on too many waterways and is one reason catch-and-release is so important. Release those big bass so they can chomp the sunnies and maintain healthier lakes. Exotic vegetation like curly-leaf pondweed and Eurasian water milfoil, which spread quickly and choke out balanced native vegetation, hasn't helped in this regard.

Because of their toughness and ability to survive in warmer water, you'll find largemouth in virtually every reservoir, river, stream, or marsh that's connected to any of our big river systems. (Walleyes inhabit many of the same waters.) Backwater areas of rivers or flooded timber provide excellent locations for finding largemouth bass. They've also been stocked just about anywhere else, including farm ponds dotted across much of America. But even though they're found in many places, we usually can locate bass in specific locations on any given waterway. It's not hard to decipher where these locations exist, so unlike other species of fish—say those oft-suspended, nomadic crappies—it's relatively easy to get efficient with your bass search.

It all boils down to one word: structure. This could mean many different things, including natural or man-made structure like flooded timber, sunken islands, riprap, or emergent vegetation like lily pads or bulrushes. In general, I've found that the more variety of habitats, the better the fishing.

Talkin' Largies

Largemouth long have been king in the southern United States, but even amateur anglers recognize that quality largemouth water exists north of the Mason-Dixon Line. The largemouth bass (*Micropterus salmoides*) grows larger than smallmouth bass and ranges much farther south—all the way into Mexico (where I've fished them) if you want to head way south. They grow larger than smallies in North Country, though not by much. The state record largemouth in my home state of Minnesota—8 pounds, 15 ounces—was caught in autumn 2005. Obviously that's a smidge smaller than George Perry's 22-pound, 4-ounce Georgia largemouth (which just marked its seventy-fifth anniversary in June 2007). The Gopher State's top smallmouth is 8 pounds, 0 ounce, so it's not much smaller than the Minnesota largemouth record. And it's not ridiculously smaller than the David Hayes world record 11-pound, 15-ounce Tennessee smallie caught in 1955.

Largemouth tend to run multiple shades of green in color and have a long, blotchy horizontal stripe running along their lateral line from gill plate to tail on both sides. I like this about largemouth—every fish looks unique and beautiful. Once you've caught enough largemouth and smallmouth bass, telling the difference between the two is ridiculously easy, but every new angler wants to understand the name difference—largemouth vs. smallmouth—so here goes. Looking at it from a profile view, the jaw of a largemouth bass is longer than on a smallmouth and stretches past the eye. On a smallie, the corner of the jaw ends rights below the eye. And, yes, when you lip-land a largemouth, its mouth does appear larger than your basic smallmouth—hence the nickname bigmouth, or bucketmouth.

Any tournament angler can tell you that in some parts of the country, largemouth grow faster and bigger thanks to a longer growing season. Even casual bassers know the largemouth record has nearly fallen a couple of times. California, with its huge warm-water reservoir fish, came close to creating a new world record in 2006 and is likely to produce the next record eventually. In my neck of the woods, most largemouth will weigh between 1 and 3 pounds, and I can find and fish bass of that size (9 to 19 inches) all day.

During winter, the warm water–loving largemouth loses it voracious appetite and becomes lethargic and much less aggressive. Spend some time reading outdoors pages and outdoors newspapers in the northern United States from February through April, and you won't see many headlines like "Top Lakes for Lunker Bass through the Ice," or "Seven Tips for Icing Bucketmouths." If bass aren't striking and fighting, we're usually not pursuing them. For that reason, largemouth bass fishing is a late-spring, summer, and early-autumn pursuit, and the hard-core anglers (yours truly) head south to warmer climes and open water to scratch that largemouth itch. (That's exactly how I caught my biggest bass ever, a double-digit specimen from Lake Amistad, Texas, in late October 2007. What a blast!) I believe many more bass these days survive a long time thanks to the growing catch-and-release ethic across the country.

Largemouth and smallmouth bass are predators; they'll eat just about any living, moving creatures they can catch: minnows, small-fry, or fingerlings, of virtually any species for breakfast; amphibians like frogs or salamanders for lunch; baitfish such as shad, small panfish or roughfish, and shiners for dinner; insects as appetizers; and crayfish for dessert. Land critters like shrews or mice and waterfowl such as ducklings in the water also are fair game for big bass. Like most creatures, however, bass prefer steady sources of forage, so they establish home territories near good feeding areas.

According to life history information on bass from the University of Minnesota, young bass eat mostly plankton and other tiny critters like waterfleas. They can put on weight fast, and in warmer southern climes they can become fishable their first year. We don't enjoy such speedy growth rates where I came of age as an angler, but during the shorter growing season in this part of the country, bass feed as actively and aggressively as anywhere else. As they grow, they move up the dining scale to the nymph stages of big insects like dragonflies, damselflies, and other bugs. Baitfish like small shad become the primary food source of adult bass, although worms, big insects, frogs, and crayfish end up in their bellies, too. Consequently, many fishing techniques we'll discuss in this book mimic these prey species.

As bass anglers, this affects how we fish, because we're trying to trick these predators into believing we're throwing food at them. Bass eat live food, and they seem to love the thrill of the chase more than other piscatorial species, which is one reason they're more fun to catch than, say, the not-so-humble walleye.

So as bass anglers we're mostly finding the natural food sources, then trying to match them via artificial offerings to garner more strikes. For example, the northern Mississippi River usually produces a good crop of baitfish every spring, so by midsummer you'd better believe I'm working flashy crankbaits at multiple depths in this waterway. In spring before much natural forage has bloomed, I'll work an artificial frog over lily pads or other matted vegetation. Rock areas, especially in clear water, with lots of nooks and crevices usually hold abundant crayfish, which largemouth and smallmouth bass alike absolutely love! There are a lot of plastics and crankbait lures that resemble crayfish—go figure!

Watching bass feed is amazing. I've seen underwater video and live bass in tanks up close, and largemouth will snap open their massive mouth and— in the blink of an eye—swallow whatever food source they're targeting. One second the baitfish is there; the next second that big old bucketmouth is sitting there with a contented look on his face. Big largemouth will consume big baitfish, which is a major reason you can use large lures when targeting largemouths. (Smallies, as a general rule, require a little more finesse.) I've seen 20-inch largemouth trying to swallow 6-inch baitfish— no kidding!

Largemouth bass target their prey a number of ways, but most largies that strike the end of my line usually are in ambush mode. They're hanging around some sort of shady structure—weeds, underwater branches or trees, or docks—and waiting for something tasty to swim past. This is especially true in late summer, when they're seeking relief from the sun and baitfish are in ample supply. Other times of year, particularly in spring, big largemouth are more likely to be patrolling the breakline or other, deeper structure for their next dinner.

Wherever I fish tournaments, when the water warms to about 60 to 65 degrees (in May and June in Minnesota), largemouth begin spawning in the shallows. Farther south, even into southern Illinois and Ohio, the bass spawn wraps up by late April most years. Multiple environmental factors trigger the spawn, and I've seen its timing vary by three weeks on a given lake from year to year. Male bass enter spawning areas to find prime nesting spots, then the females follow and drop thousands of eggs (according to professional fisheries reports, like the University of Minnesota's) in an area the male clears. He then guards the eggs, which hatch in a few days (depending on region), from panfish and other pesky predators.

Most states in the northern United States close the season for largemouth bass around the spawn to protect the fish from overzealous anglers. These fish are very susceptible to harvest during the spawn because they'll protect the nest at all costs. It may be great fun pulling that aggressive male off the nest with a flashy lure, but if the local panfish come gobble all the eggs while you're releasing him, you're hurting the next generation of bass and bass anglers! For that reason, I strongly urge all bass anglers, professional and amateur, North and South, to avoid fishing bass on the beds! When the young bass, called fry, hatch from the eggs, the male will hang around with them until they go their separate ways within a few days. It's tough out there for the fry—everything is trying to eat them—which is a major reason that mama bass produces so many eggs.

Just via simple visual observation, it's clear when the spawn is occurring on a given lake or reservoir. Once it starts, the spawn usually wraps up in a couple weeks in North Country because water can warm up through that prime spawning temperature range pretty fast. After the spawn, females especially can be difficult to catch because they're pretty hung over from the spawning process. Perhaps the females of any species can relate (I certainly can): We just want to be left alone! Within a couple of weeks, however, they're hungry again, and some of the best bass fishing of the year will commence.

A Basic Largemouth Search

The classic largemouth scenario probably breaks down like this: You're running your trolling motor from the front of your casting platform while casting into the weedy shallows that ring the shoreline. Behind you, the water gets deeper and the emergent, and eventually submergent, vegetation disappears. The shallow flats in front of you offer incredible foraging opportunities and spawning locations for early and late in the open-water season, but the deep water provides a more constant, temperate zone where bass, especially big bass, can find consistent temperatures during the extremes of the year—i.e., late summer and winter.

Find the "deep holes" where current, dredging, or the lake's natural formation has carved out a deep bottom, and you've probably found a prime zone for big fish seeking relief from extreme heat or cold. I won't call the deep flats "no fish land," but generally speaking, that's the last place I'll search for largemouth on lakes. Offshore structure could include a hump or emergent flats where bass may be holding on top or along the sides. As we'll discuss later, modern electronics, especially a GPS in tandem with some sort of contour mapping technology, can make researching such structure much easier.

When fishing the shallows, we're looking for specific types of areas that hold bass, and a common problem for anglers here is too much quality structure. Examples include submerged brush or other woody vegetation, points or small peninsulas that jut into the main lake basin (especially rocky points), or the slackwater areas with vegetation near some current. Moving water usually carries baitfish or other food sources, and largemouth love to be near such areas, ready to strike.

If I'm fishing a tournament on a reservoir situation—say, Lake Pepin on the Mississippi River—you're likely to find me working rocky riprap areas near culverts or just downstream of where a creek enters the lake. Too much good structure? This is one reason bass anglers have a reputation for moving a lot, because we're going to sample all of that good structure; if any one doesn't produce quickly, we're going to move on, fast! Look for areas that really stand out from surrounding lake contours or substrate, and try them first.

In between the shallows and the deep flats is the all-important breakline. This transition zone, which is almost like a mini-continental shelf (to make a saltwater analogy), marks the point where the shallow flats quickly drop off into deeper water. (Hint: When fishing a new lake, look for places on your contour map where the water gets deep fast.) Light disappears as the water deepens, so vegetation disappears, too. The breakline provides a corridor where bass will travel to other points of structure, as well as a safe area where bass may hold early and late in the day.

If casting the shallows is Bassin' 101 at the University of Fishing, then working a finesse worm off the breakline is Bassin' 201. Many seasoned bass anglers start at the breakline, especially early in the day before the shallows begin warming up. Watch for largemouth to congregate in the "inside turn" areas of a breakline where it forms a shallow bowl adjacent to a bay or corner of the shoreline. Combine an inside turn of a breakline with some simple structure, like green weeds early in the year, and you've got an absolute prime largemouth honey hole.

Classic deepwater locations for me usually mean finding some sort of submerged rocks or man-made structure (like fish cribs) that doesn't appear on any lake maps. These can run deeper than you might expect. I've pulled largemouth up from 15 or even 20 feet off a deep, rocky reef. Other places may be where some light current has slowly created an underwater edge that even the latest lake mapmaker hasn't located. Prime spots usually are near a sharp transition to a shallow area where big bass can feed, but then quickly retreat to the safety of deep water when fishing pressure or some other environmental factor drives them out of the shallows.

When I see such situations on a contour map, I'll use my depthfinder or my underwater video camera to scan it. Inevitably, there's something down there—a rock pile, an underwater hump, or a submerged bridge—where bass will stack up. Finding something like this is really exciting. I feel like a detective searching for clues, and when I find a spot like this, it makes my day! In a tournament situation, I'll always use my GPS to mark this structure and begin working around its edges. Any blips on the depthfinder that show unique structure along those edges usually represent what we bass loyalists call the "spot on a spot," and you'd better believe I'll fish that spot hard!

Farther north, on the edge of the largemouth's range, you'll sometimes encounter incredibly fast drop-offs just a few feet from the rocky shorelines of Canadian Shield–type waters. In case you haven't already noticed, bass love rocks, and even steep wall-like rocky structure will attract cruising bass. Southern bass gurus in Missouri and other locales know this rule, too. They'll often work the rocky limestone caves that jut underwater and provide that all-important shade for big, hungry bucketmouths.

Strictly Smallies

Smallmouth identification is easy after a little time on the water. When in doubt, check out the jaw. Note how its back corner ends below the eye. A largemouth's jaw extends to behind the eye. MITCH KEZAR, WINDIGOIMAGES.COM

Now let's talk strictly smallmouth (*Micropterus dolomieu*), otherwise known as bronzebacks across most of their range. Bronzebacks have received that moniker thanks to their tanner, almost brownish color, and—though they can appear greenish, too—smallies always lack those distinctly dark horizontal markings along the lateral line that you see on a largemouth.

Quite the opposite, smallmouth have dark vertical bars that can appear every ½ inch or so along the fish's length. Their presence, or lack thereof, seems to vary from waterway to waterway. As I explained earlier, when in doubt, the back edge of the jaw stops right below the eye on a smallie; it does not extend beyond it as on a largemouth. Trust me, after you catch a few, bass ID is like cats and dogs.

That's despite the fact that smallmouth can show some remarkable color variation. Stress can change the color of almost any fish, and this rule truly applies to smallmouth. During the spawn on Lake Mille Lacs in central Minnesota, I've seen smallies look almost black. Keep any fish out of the water too long, and its brilliant colors will fade.

Generally you're going to find smallmouth in cooler, clearer water than the largemouth, although many lakes and rivers contain both species. They're found in the southern United States, too, but their range ends at much more northerly climes than the largemouth, extending deeper into Canada than Mr. Bucketmouth. In portions of the Upper Midwest, you'll find smallmouth in some of the same streams and rivers where you find brown trout. For that reason, smallmouth have become quite popular with the fly-angling set, and there's a nifty little subculture of anglers who use driftboats on big rivers or float-tube on small rivers while fly-casting for lunker smallmouth. Tie into a 3-pound smallie with a 5-weight fly rod and you're in for some exciting fishing!

Though they have a well-deserved reputation for preferring moving water, you'll find smallies in many northern lakes and reservoirs, especially with hard, sandy bottoms. To provide food and fishing sport, many smallmouth were stocked into cold border country lakes 100-plus years ago where they had never previously existed. For that reason, many visitors from places like Minnesota's Boundary Waters Canoe Area Wilderness have pictures of themselves hoisting up lunker, red-eyed smallmouth. A good rule of thumb: If you find robust smallmouth in a lake or river, you're probably fishing pretty healthy, clean water. I've caught them all across the central and eastern portions of the United States, including the Mississippi drainage, the St. Lawrence River, the Great Lakes, and a personal favorite smallmouth destination, New York/Vermont's Lake Champlain. (We'll talk more about those locations later.)

Smallmouth grow slower than largemouth, thanks partially to living in cooler, slower growing environments. But smallmouth simply don't grow as large as their bigmouth cousins, although you can catch many from 1 to 3 pounds across their range. Tennessee produced the world-record smallie, which weighed 11 pounds, 15 ounces and measured 27 inches long.

Because they're a cooler-water species, smallmouth demand more care with catch-and-release. I make sure my live well is very well oxygenated and as cool as possible before placing any fish into it, especially smallmouth. When practicing catch-and-release, please snap pictures quickly of your smallies, then quickly return them to the water. They're a hair more fragile than their bigmouth cousins, in my experience.

Predators like the largemouth, young smallmouth first consume plankton, then insects, working their way up to baitfish toward the end of their first summer. The classic smallmouth prey is crayfish, and I've caught many smallmouth over the years that are regurgitating these claw-snapping crustaceans. Perhaps it's because in a colder environment, smallmouth must be more versatile in targeting prey species, but even more so than largemouth bass, smallmouth love smacking topwater lures, a technique we'll describe more later. Because they live in more northerly locations, they spawn later than largies and in slightly cooler water—often getting motivated with nest building when water temperatures are in the high 50s.

Do I prefer smallmouth to largemouth or vice versa? I love them both; though, if forced to choose, I'd definitely say smallmouth, simply because they're symbolic of the wonderful cool lakes, rivers, and streams in the portion of the country where I grew up. There's just something about these feisty little brown bass that is utterly addictive. Outside the trout and salmon family, they probably fight harder pound for pound than any other freshwater fish. One second a large smallmouth is burrowing your lure into the sediment under the boat, and the next he's breaking water and sizzling line off your reel. In my part of the country, many anglers can recount their first success story with a big smallmouth; the species inspires young and old alike.

Here's a little secret about smallmouth that most tournament folks would never give away: Smallies are curious little buggers that notice anything out of place. That's why simple techniques like deadsticking (i.e., leaving a lure lying on the bottom or topwater, then maybe just twitching it occasionally) drive smallmouth nuts. Leave a lure in their neighborhood long enough, and they just can't resist!

Smallmouth Locations

Smallmouth locations are very much like largemouth locations, although they demand higher water quality, which eliminates them from a good chunk of the largemouth's range. They prefer a harder bottom than largemouth, and they're willing to stay in deeper water longer than their larger cousins to find the bottom structure and safety zone they demand. Smallies love rocks even more than largemouth bass, especially large boulders that cast some shade. Some of the best football-size smallmouth locations on Lake Mille Lacs in central Minnesota feature just a few big rocks or small boulders in 7 or 8 feet of water.

Where you have rocks and clear, cool water, you probably have crayfish. These mini-"lobsters" provide a nutritious food source for bass (particularity smallies), which consider them culinary delights. Try working such areas with crankbaits that mimic crayfish. MITCH KEZAR, WINDIGOIMAGES.COM

To summarize, smallmouth are more finicky, and smart bass anglers use this trait to their advantage. You need four key elements for smallmouth: a clean environment, shade, forage, and the availability of both deep- and shallow-water habitats. Find that spot, say a rocky bar or clump of vegetation, that contains smallmouth, and mark it in your GPS. Odds are that many lunker-smallmouth anglers know the spot. (This is also a reason smallmouth catch-and-release is so important! Once anglers locate these places, it's all too easy to really hammer these slow-growing fish.)

Even in weedy areas, smallmouth want to stay over a hard bottom. Mucky-bottom areas on warmer, what seasoned anglers and biologists call "eutrophic," lakes (where algae blooms occur or nonnative exotics like milfoil thrive) rarely contain smallmouth bass. It's those low-nutrient, coldwater, "oligotrophic" lakes with long sandy or rocky bottoms areas that we want to work for smallmouth. Find me a big old white pine toppled over a hard-sloping, gravelling bottom over a clear-water lake, and I'll catch you a smallmouth bass, every time!

Earlier, I mentioned finding steep rocky outcroppings in Canadian Shield waters for the northernmost largemouth bass. Well, if you're too far north for largies, I can almost guarantee you'll pull a big smallmouth from a rocky gap or underwater ledge. If I can leave the novice angler with one simple rule for smallies, it's this: Find the rocks!

CHAPTER TWO

Influences on Success

The Mother Nature Factor

Once you succeed (or think you've succeeded) in understanding basic bass fishing locations, Mother Nature throws you a wicked curve ball. We can summarize that nasty pitch in one word: weather. Everything I just explained about bass haunts and locations depends on a fairly stable weather pattern. That translates into consistent temperatures and clear skies or a few high clouds. Seems like most of this decade, for whatever reason, the only thing constant about the weather is change. I rarely plan a tournament around a stable weather pattern, and the first thing I check before heading to an event is the weather report. Like I said, I expect something, but the severity and type of weather can change my plans and determine what locations I'll work on a given body of water.

Bass become significantly less predictable before, during, and after a weather front. The change in air pressure, temperature, and disturbance to the water column from additional direct rain, wind, or runoff all can affect the position and mood of the fish. Think about it: Their entire environment has changed—they can't go indoors like you or I—so it's no surprise that they act a little weird. In my experience, bass of all sorts throw on the feedbag prior to a front's arrival, but no two words frustrate tournament anglers more than "cold front." There's not a tournament angler alive who hasn't enjoyed excellent prefishing before an event, only to have an early summer cold front shut down the bite.

Animals can sense impending weather changes better than humans, and prior to a storm is a great time to be on the water chucking something aggressive. Usually, however, Murphy's Law demands that day one of a tournament opens about six hours after a front arrives, when the bass aren't feeding or active. Later we'll talk about a finesse approach, and here's one time that demands it.

The most common weather factor that will challenge almost any angler is wind, and let me be frank here: I hate wind! Novice (and not-so-novice) fly-anglers and spinning-reel users alike struggle with casting and proper lure placement in windy conditions. Casting into a breeze is an exercise in frustration, so whenever possible, position yourself or your boat so you're casting with the wind. (You'll be amazed how much farther you can cast!) Boat control also becomes more difficult, so mastering your trolling-motor technique will help in properly positioning your watercraft. In really high winds, the resulting rough water can become hazardous, and on big lakes (or even small lakes) I simply won't fish if the overall weather conditions become too dangerous. No event, or fish, is worth risking my life.

Wind also can alter the behavior and location of the fish, but we can use that fact to our advantage. A windblown shoreline almost works like a stream, river, or any other place with current. Tip: With any type of fishing, water with some turbulence (think "stirring") contains food that attracts big fish like bass. Walleye guys know this tip well, too, and in the right conditions this can produce phenomenal fishing. We'll get into specific lures and tactics later, but these windblown shorelines are good places to toss spinnerbaits or—if you know the water is deep enough—even crankbaits.

Rain (and sometimes snow at my really early-season tournament events) often accompanies wind. Downpours aren't fun to fish under, but in my experience light rain or stalled-out gray skies usually help the fishing. Spend enough time outdoors and you'll appreciate recreating under clouds rather than a beating-hot sun. When wind or heavy rain gets so severe that you begin to feel unsafe on the water, tell yourself this: You're probably not missing prime fishing. The fish feel the same way about the turbid, unstable water conditions and have bailed out of the shallows. In my experience, they're off to spend two or three days in a deepwater funk.

Here's a windy silver lining: While avoiding wind in my prime locations, I've discovered some great new fishing spots that I otherwise never would have found. Even on tough weather days, you probably can find a hidden bay or inlet sheltered enough to safely drop a line. Over time, you'll develop windy-day options, and these same spots—which you probably ignored before—might become prime water even under clear skies.

Boating Equipment

Bass are a popular species to fish for many reasons, but one is that—thanks to the sheer luck of evolution—they're found virtually everywhere in the country. They're aggressive, hungry, and love the shallows, so citizens of all backgrounds and income levels can enjoy catching this fish. Part of the beauty of catching bucketmouths is that you don't need a boat. Millions of people in this country enjoy fishing bass from shore, from float tubes, or from other small watercraft not considered classic "bass boats." Back when my children were smaller, my husband and I would take them to Cedar Lake outside Annandale, Minnesota. I'd spend hours on a windsurfing board (minus the sail) kicking around the breakline fishing bass. Our family dog at the time would sun himself on the bow, providing a nice balancing counterweight while I fished.

Though I firmly believe you can fish bass from shore all day, sometimes chasing this species means working big water. Perhaps you'll develop into a serious bass angler and consider the tournament scene. Whatever the reason, many recreational anglers often ask me about my boat, so in this section I want to describe what qualifies as the perfect bass rig for Karen Savik.

If you've got a fat checkbook, you can spend as much as you want on a bass boat. Some folks go overboard spending-wise, but there are basic features that make a boat more practical for this style of fishing. On small water, virtually any shallow-hulled craft will suffice. One of my friends who grew up along the Upper Mississippi River fished his entire youth making short multispecies trips on a flat-bottom aluminum duck-hunting boat.

The first time he fished in my fiberglass V-hull, he sat amazed. "Wow, I didn't know you could ride over waves like this and not feel your spine being crushed," he said. Yeah, any boat will do, but if you're going to spend serious weeks every summer targeting bass, invest in a more comfortable experience.

I fish a 20-foot fiberglass, shallow V-hull with a 96-inch (8-foot) beam powered by a 225-horse Evinrude E-Tech. Here's why that works for me. Glass boats run a little quieter than aluminum rigs, though you're going to spend more for fiberglass. They're heavier, but again, I like the smoothness and the variability in fiberglass hulls, in terms of design and length. Why the V-hull? Well, unlike my friend's flat-bottom, which—to its credit—went anywhere in those Mississippi River backwaters via a Go-Devil motor on the stern, a V-hull cuts through the waves and delivers a much smoother ride. That's important for a tournament angler like me who covers miles of water every day, though even rank-and-file fishermen and women will appreciate the comfort. That said, the key word in "shallow V-hull" is "shallow." You still want to access those weedy bays and lily pads where a deep-V walleye rig would bottom out. Hence the shallow-draft bass boat: the best of both worlds!

Bass anglers are casters. We like clearance, serious boat control, and an unencumbered view—i.e., low gunwales and an open casting platform. Standing around, talking, and casting on a bluebird day is a key reason I love bass fishing so much, and I suspect there are a lot of people just like me. The classic bass boat has evolved from these demands. Wind can't push the low-profile hull of a bass boat around as much as a deeper V-hull walleye rig, and those low gunwales mean a clearer view (and shot) for casting. As for that wide, 8-foot beam, it's a tight fit in the garage, but I like the space for gear storage compartments and my casting platform. Narrower bows may look big enough, but put yourself up there with a trolling motor, a depthfinder, and a tackle box, and you'll catch yourself tripping over gear. Even at that width, I'll catch myself thumping into my bump seat up front. Make sure you can move that (incredibly handy) bump seat when you don't feel like sitting or leaning against it.

As a tournament angler, this girl hits some big water, and I simply feel more comfortable in a 20-foot boat running over big waves than in an 18-footer or smaller. Wind can change in an instant, and when rough weather rolls in, that 225-horse motors me back to shore fast. Though you're more

Opposite: I fish a 20-foot fiberglass, shallow V-hull with a 96-inch beam powered by a 225-horsepower Evinrude E-Tech. MITCH KEZAR, WINDIGOIMAGES.COM

likely to encounter potentially dangerous water on the Great Lakes, which I fish several times per year, it can happen on smaller lakes or rivers, too.

Lake Mille Lacs in central Minnesota, for example, has excellent smallmouth fishing. Many, many anglers in the Gopher State can share some frightening stories about "big rollers" on this 13-mile-wide lake. And don't believe anyone who says you can't fish docks in a 20-foot boat; I do it all the time. If you're fishing small, 1,500-acre lakes and reservoirs and never anticipate fishing serious big water, a 14- or 16-footer will suffice. Avoid going much smaller than that. Here's why.

Bass anglers like stuff. We own multiple tackle boxes, dozens of rods, all-weather gear for any circumstance, electronics many people can't even pronounce, and accessories galore! You're going to want a boat with storage containers, plus that wide casting platform. You'll want a live well, preferably an insulated one to keep fish cool on hot days, with an

When bass fishing becomes an addiction, like it has for me, you will find yourself in desperate need of storage space for all the lures and other "essential" gear you have purchased. When you take the plunge and buy yourself a serious bass boat, make sure it has ample storage for all your tackle. MITCH KEZAR, WINDIGOIMAGES.COM

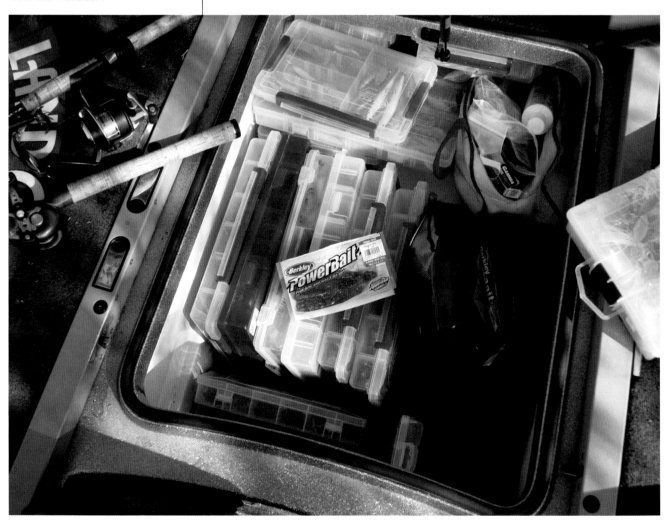

aerator. (Even when I intend to release a fish, I throw it in the live well to reinvigorate it in the oxygen-rich water for a little while.)

Other mandatory equipment includes a bow-mounted trolling motor and a couple of depthfinders—one in the console and one by my trolling motor. An automatic bilge pump keeps water out of your craft, and an onboard charger attaches to your batteries and ensures that they're charging when you plug it in at night. Every boat should be properly outfitted with lights, mostly to help other boats avoid you. I fish bass frequently at dusk, so I'm constantly checking and monitoring my lights. My ideal boat also has a lot of rod locker storage (to hold at least twelve rods), plus other spare compartments for a lot of gear. I like it manageable, not plumb full. Most people these days rely on cell phones and Blackberries for monitoring weather more than all-weather radios, but it's still a good idea to have a quality radio running, especially on big water.

By the way, the water pressure gauge is the most important dial on that console. Boat manufacturers put a massive rock-and-roll speedometer on the console (which rarely works), then an itty-bitty water pressure gauge. Personally, I'm way more interested in whether my motor is getting enough water to cool it than whether I can run faster than the next guy. (I usually

It is important to have two aerated live wells that keep the fish alive and happy. It also provides plenty of room for that great catch. MITCH KEZAR, WINDIGOIMAGES.COM

can monitor my speed via the RPM or GPS reading anyway.) This angler is not a "need for speed" kind of gal, but I like that big horsepower when it's necessary. As a tournament angler, you never know when you'll need to head in quick for a weigh-in or to avoid nasty weather.

I'm also hearing more questions on multibladed props. I still prefer a three-blade prop because it gives me more top-end speed when I'm covering water. You lose a couple miles per hour with four- and five-blade props, but they give you that initial burst of speed that some tournament guys prefer at shotgun-start events, or for taking off in shallow water.

As for trailers, a couple of quick thoughts: Backing up is easier with a single-axle trailer, but bigger boats, like my own, require a tandem axle. Bottom line: Make sure when you buy a boat that you have plenty of motor and trailer to support it. I will add that trailers with steps are great; that's a fabulous idea that should have been thought of long ago!

Fishing Electronics

Although bass anglers don't rely on electronics as much as the average walleye angler, they're still very important. But electronics intimidate beginning anglers for a couple of reasons. First, if you're unfamiliar with them, they look pretty complicated. Second, you can spend a lot of money on them. Let's dispel those notions quickly. The average angler can buy simple electronics that encompass 90-plus percent of the top-of-the-line models' basic functions at an affordable price, and you can learn to use them quickly. Yes, you catch fish without electronics, but you'll become more efficient, and frankly have more fun, with a couple of these devices in your bass-fishing tool kit.

The depthfinder is the one piece of fishing electronics I absolutely would not fish without. There are many styles and price ranges, but bottom line, this device tells you (at least) the depth of the water you're fishing. A depthfinder reveals the humps and structure underneath your boat to provide a clear view of the bottom content, and this information correlates directly to which type of presentation you should employ. Want a clear view of the breakline or structure that could hold bass? A quality depthfinder can unveil every nook and cranny. Via a transducer, depthfinders relay a good old-fashioned sonar signal off the bottom to provide an accurate

depth reading. Simple round dial–style flashers run a little cheaper and offer some insight into whether large fish or baitfish are present. They don't, however, provide a history of what happened 5 yards back, so if you're distracted when you pass over a large fish, a flasher won't tell you what you missed. I keep one in my boat, however, because they seem to provide more accurate depth readings when I'm scouting at higher speeds. I also believe they show more consistent readings through thick weeds.

What you need is a liquid crystal display graph, which shows you an actual picture on a miniscreen of the water your boat has passed over, including crisp Vs or delineations showing fish. Anglers new to LCD graphs often misinterpret what they're seeing, but with experience, you'll be amazed at the detail and specific underwater information one of these devices can provide. For monitoring bottom structure, you can't beat a multidimensional picture, and that's just what an LCD graph illustrates. High-resolution, color-display graphs have been dropping in price in recent years and have become the standard on the LCD market. Most

Today's liquid-crystal graphs combine depthfinder technology with GPS and lake map data to create an absolutely indispensable unit for any angler. Prices have dropped to the point that just about anyone can justify the expense. MITCH KEZAR, WINDIGOIMAGES.COM mark fish at ridiculously deep depths, way beyond the needs of most bass anglers. If you get seriously into fishing, you'll want both a flasher and an LCD, and these days you really don't even need to choose. There are many combo units on the market with split screens, with a flasher bar on one side of the LCD screen, or you can switch between the two with a flick of a button. If you want to spend even more, there are many units that combine sonar and GPS, which I'll talk about shortly.

When you buy a unit, consider the cone angle of the transducer—the device that concentrates that sonar sound into a beam. Imagine a cone with the tip starting at the transducer, then widening as the water deepens, and you'll better understand this concept. It's the area the sonar wave covers. A transducer with a narrower cone angle concentrates the signal, which translates into better resolution on the screen. The better the resolution, the better information you have on what's swimming below—maybe a lunker hawg. The trade-off with great resolution is that you see a narrower area and miss marking potentially big fish nearby. That's why LCD manufacturers sell multibeam transducers: one (or more) for a wide view and one for a narrow, higher res view. One practical rule of thumb to remember here is that the shallower the water, the smaller the cone angle. Finally, these units really have dropped in price since I started fishing. A quick Web search revealed fine black-and-white models for a couple hundred dollars. You can even buy little hand-held models for backcountry fishing.

When you begin getting serious about bass fishing from a boat, invest in a good depthfinder. Obviously, multitransducer models cost more, and the sky is the limit on features and gadgets with high-end models. I don't use half the bells and whistles on my depthfinder, but any unit in my boat will have a water temperature gauge, and I make sure its gain (sensitivity) is easily adjustable. Bottom line: A depthfinder will take your fishing to the next level—you'll see and investigate more structure that you wouldn't know existed without it. You can get better deals on closeout model "fish finders" during late summer or fall, and a sport show is a great place to see dozens, or even hundreds, of units in one place and get some hands-on learning with one.

New and improved depthfinders hit the market every year with all sort of added gadgets and features, even though its basic function as a sonar unit hasn't changed much. Another facet on the electronics scene has changed dramatically for the better the past ten or twelve years, though—Global

Positioning System (GPS) units. These devices triangulate information from the U.S. government's satellite systems to tell you your exact position to the nearest few feet, and they've improved tremendously in accuracy and reliability since I began using them fifteen years ago. You can buy battery-powered handheld or mounted, large-screen LCD graphlike models, even units that incorporate other features, like depthfinders.

GPS serves two primary navigation features: For starters, although it's less of a concern if you're fishing a small lake or pond down the road, GPS has an important safety role when fishing big water. Many big-water boaters and anglers around the world rely on GPS to help navigate them home (and through safe water) when low-visibility weather arrives. I wouldn't participate in a Great Lakes or any other big-water tournament event without my GPS. To be frank, even on calm days, GPS has helped lead me through some confusing stretches of water. (I once fished an event south of New Orleans that had a dizzying number of inlets, islands, side channels, and peninsulas that all looked the same to me. I'd still be slowly wandering through those bayous if it weren't for my GPS!) Handheld units are handy because you can use them for hiking or other non-boat-related activities, but I love my mounted model with its wide, easy-to-read screen and steady power supply from my boat's batteries.

As for fishing, you can plug specific waypoint coordinates into a GPS unit so that you can return to that same spot again and again. If you're willing to spend more money, you can buy units that incorporate maps of specific lakes, complete with structure and depth contours. Many tournament anglers plot likely points to investigate on an upcoming event on their home computer, then upload them to their GPS before even leaving home. The dominant trend in fishing electronics today is combining features within one unit.

The underwater camera hit the fishing scene like a whirlwind in the late 1990s, and many anglers use them for year-round fishing. A cable connects the underwater camera to the main unit and a small viewing screen in the boat. I keep one in my boat for those times when I want to get a direct look at the bottom content, structure, or even a fish that's frustrating me by refusing to bite. You're not going to get a plasma TV–like picture of anything, but you can't argue with the proof of actual sight and direct video. That said, buy a depthfinder and GPS unit first when you take your wallet to the fishing electronics section of your favorite sporting goods store.

CHAPTER THREE

Hitting the Water

Casting Tips

OK, let's start thinking about getting our line in the water. Casting is more than effectively dropping a lure into the sweet spot. Different styles of casting and—more importantly—retrieves create different angles that can present the same lure in very different ways. More than once while fishing, I've thrown a lure with nary a sniff, then cast so that it lands and runs at a different angle—and watched in amused disbelief as a big bass swallows it whole.

To cast successfully, your equipment—rod, reel, line, and lure—must be properly balanced. The occasional angler need not become too hung up on this, but to truly maximize the potential of the many often subtle techniques described in these pages, you need control over your cast. And that usually means balanced equipment. It starts with the lure, and the rule of thumb is: The heavier the lure, the stouter the rod. That's one reason tournament anglers own so many rods.

Sure, they could cast huge lures on ultralight equipment, and vice versa, but for precise casts, this tournament girl tries to match rod and lure as perfectly as possible. Don't worry; you don't need two dozen rods rigged with every style of lure in every action. Tournament folks operate that way because rerigging during fishing time can cost them fish. The average bass enthusiast can cover all his or her bases with three or four rods ranging in length from 6 feet to a 7-footer in increasing actions. We'll discuss which rod when in the presentation section.

As for casting, when you're looking for serious distance and the prospect of a louder splash doesn't bother you, go with the basic but powerful overhand cast, which maximizes the loading power of a given rod. If there's a piece of structure that I can cast past safely, I have no problem with the fast-and-dirty overhand cast. Bring the handle to about a twelve o'clock position, allow the rod a second to load behind you, then bring your hand quickly forward to a ten o'clock position. After the lure splashes down, I'll usually let it sit until the ripples dissipate, then begin my retrieve to alleviate the initial shock of the splash.

With a sidearm cast, you lose some of your rod's loading power, but it allows you to reach those spots where the overhand cast has no chance. "Skipping docks," where we're literally sneaking the lure under a horizontal structure, is a classic example. Get your body as low as possible, then, in simple terms, make a light overhand cast with your arm at 90 degrees (perpendicular) to your body. It's super-easy; the hardest part is control—

I use these great Fenwick rods and reels for ten to twelve hours a day, five to seven days per week. Make sure they are light and sensitive. MITCH KEZAR, WINDIGOIMAGES.COM

not tossing it with too much force. Finesse people, finesse! Another well-known "skipping" cast technique involves a quick wrist flick rather than a full-armed casting motion.

Flipping and pitching are subtle but more technical casting techniques that lend themselves best to jigs or Texas-rigged plastics. Your goal: to quietly enter holes, heavy cover, or turbid water to find lethargic bass. Flipping has become especially popular, or at least necessary, in lakes heavily infested with milfoil. Huge, thick mats of this exotic plant hold bass, which especially seem to appreciate its shade during late summer's heat, but it's next to impossible to retrieve anything through the thick stuff. Flipping evolved among savvy bassers, and it's a simple concept.

Quietly take your boat into the milfoil areas, and watch for holes or spaces in the vegetation combined with some sort of structure. There should be a lot of them, and they're typically where bass await their next meal, especially in midsummer, when the milfoil is lush and really growing. With your boat perched 12 to 15 feet away, let out anywhere from 12 to 18 feet of line, then grab the line (closed bail) by your rod's first line guide and pull as much back as possible. Then simply swing your lure close to surface toward the hole you want to fish, releasing the line in your hand as you do so. This takes a little practice (it's all in the wrist!) to become pinpoint accurate, but overall it's a simple, quiet technique.

In my experience, bass will often grab your jig-and-pig or rig on the drop or just as your begin your retrieve, so be ready to take up your slack quickly. If nothing strikes, try bouncing it a few times before retrieving it. Flipping doesn't excite most bass anglers as much as the image of big largemouth nailing a burning spinnerbait, but it's effective, and many tournament anglers have won events because flipping the foil worked when nothing else performed. The basic casting motion of flipping also works well with some surface lures, like artificial frogs or silver minnows that you'll drag over lilies or matted weeds.

Pitching is an actual open-bail cast, with more of a shooting motion that allows you to fire the lure under docks or low-hanging branches. And though it's more complicated than flipping, you can target farther spots. Release enough line so that your free hand can hold your lure about even with the reel. Place a little tension on the line, then, while moving the rod tip toward the hot spot, release the lure from your hand. The combination of tension and sweep from your rod provides the lure's forward momentum.

Get good with this technique, and you can quietly drop a lure into a choice location up to 30 feet out.

Since you're often retrieving lures farther, pitching usually works better in water with less dense vegetation. Both methods perform anywhere, anytime that stealth is a driving factor—say during night fishing—and even in clear water. My flippin' and pitchin' tactics increase later into midsummer, when largemouth and smallmouth alike already have seen the greatest hits of bass lures and are becoming increasingly skittish. Both require a medium-heavy, 7-foot-plus rod and heavy braided line to pull fish out quickly after the hookset.

With all your casting, don't be afraid to practice on the water, or even in the backyard. Pull the trebles off an old crankbait or rig a plastic sans hooks, then mess around on the lawn with some old line. Our time on the water is precious, so a little practice over the green grass of spring is time well spent. Just replace your line when you're done; any nicks or excessive dirt (which will foul your reel) can cost you a fish later.

Bass Presentations

Let me step out on a limb here and make a bold statement: No species of fish demands that anglers become more versatile with their techniques as black bass. Think about it! With muskies, you're mostly trolling or casting. Walleyes are a jigging, live-bait rigging, or crankbait special—either trolling or casting. Panfish, though many magazine articles and purists are diversifying, remain a jig, hook, and/or live-bait program. OK, now consider bass. There's finesse rigging, pitching and flipping, crankbaiting and spinnerbaiting, topwater, jig-and-pigging, spooning, drop-shotting … hell, virtually any technique that other freshwater anglers employ for their species of choice, you can use for fishing bass!

So many factors can determine which bass fishing presentation to use at any given time. Weather, time of year, the type of water, depth, and clarity: It's almost mind-boggling, even from someone who has fished tournaments for nearly fifteen years. Looking back at these past few sentences, I think I've ably summarized why bass fishing is so much fun. Later we'll talk about how to tackle those intangible factors we all encounter while bass fishing.

So without further ado, how about we tear into the meat and potatoes of bass fishing and talk tactics. I'll start with the basics: classic plastic worm rigging.

Plastics Rigging

OK, let's talk rubber worms or, more accurately in today's world, the plastic worm—or, in old-school talk, the rubber worm. They're not much to look at—although they do come in thousands of pretty colors and shapes—but no lure/presentation is more important in bass fishing than the plastic worm. They're relatively cheap, can be rigged multiple ways, and generations of bass have just loved their lifelike movement and natural-feeling, pliable bodies.

Let's get some terminology straight here first: A number of lures fall into the category of plastics, including grubs and tubes. A worm looks pretty much like a real nightcrawler with color variations. When you hear a bass angler refer to a "grub," she means the curly-tailed-style plastic like a Mr. Twister. A tube jig has a thick, bullet-nosed, hollow body with a bunch of squiggly legs dangling off the back. They're available in multiple sizes, depending on the aggressiveness of the fish, and with the new scented offerings from companies likely Berkley, fish like the way plastics smell, too. And unlike a crawler, which will squirm off your hook and provide at most a one-hit presentation, you can often fish the same plastic worm, grub, or tube for hours. Fishing a wilderness lake where bass, smallies especially, have never encountered a scented plastic worm is almost unfair—it's that effective. Plastic "worm" is probably too narrow a definition, because they come in many sizes and shapes: salamander, crayfish, leeches, frogs, and whatever else lure manufacturers' imaginations can conjure up.

A great trait about plastics is that bass don't become conditioned to these lures as quickly as most other hardbaits. On some urban, heavily fished metro lakes, I know anglers that use virtually nothing but a finesse worm for that very reason. They're also arguably the most versatile presentation available to bass anglers; they can be fished in weeds, off docks, or "swum" anywhere in the water column.

Because they tend to lose their action in colder water, plastic rigs remain first a warm-water presentation, though that's not to say they're ineffective in cold or cooling water. Unlike a spinnerbait or crankbait that sends a pulse through the water to the fish's lateral line, bass attack a plastic worm

Opposite: Every effective bass angler in America can probably hoist a handful of plastic worms, grubs, and tubes. Bass seem to become conditioned to hard baits, especially by late summer. Properly rigged finesse worms produce bass in all seasons in every region of the country. MITCH KEZAR, WINDIGOIMAGES.COM

simply because they see its forage-imitating action and want to consume it. Therefore, plastics rigging will perform best in clear or stained water (where bass can see it), not turbid farm ponds.

The basic plastic worm rig employs an offset long-shanked hook, pressed in through the top of the plastic, then flipped with the point of the hook ever so slightly reinserted into the meaty portion of the worm. This creates the "ah-ha" moment with a plastic worm: It's now weedless. (OK, pretty weedless.) You can cast it out and jig it back through light weeds, or virtually anywhere else, without getting hung up. Of course it's never quite that simple, but with practice you'll be amazed at how you're able to avoid picking up weeds with this presentation.

Add a ³⁄₁₆- to ³⁄₈-ounce bullet-headed sinker (you can modify it with a toothpick jammed between the sinker hole and line if you want to prevent it from moving; useful in some situations), and you've got what's known as a Texas rig. Don't ask me why it's called that. If it's a screw-in sinker, we bassin' folks call it a Florida rig. Move the weight up with a 15- to 30-inch leader between it and the plastic, and it's called a Carolina rig. The former (Texas) performs better in heavier cover, since that weight is near the plastic. In light cover such as shallow, grassy weeds, Carolina rigs perform well thanks to that added bit of movement. Another important function of the Carolina rig is to allow the angler to present the bait at a controlled distance above the lake bottom. In the same situation, you can also employ a basic jighead.

Place a glass bead between your hook and sinker, and you've got what bass pros call a doodle rig. The clicking and clacking of the glass bead helps generate reaction strikes from lethargic fish. Because you're looking to irritate the fish, a long slow retrieve—just inch that baby along—helps to prompt strikes. Technical tip: Learn to be a line watcher. Watch your line all the time, and you'll begin to recognize the subtle differences of how the line reacts to the bottom, to snags, and, most importantly, to fish. This rule applies more to plastics rigging that any other style of bass fishing. Wearing sensitive gloves and putting a finger on your line helps in this regard, too.

Start with larger 7- to 10-inch worms (with a 3/0 or 4/0 hook) when fishing largemouths and smaller 5- to 7-inch worms (and smaller hooks) for smallies. When you see or hear the term "finesse worm," we're talking about smaller, typically darker colored plastic rigs that finicky,

less-aggressive fish are willing to pursue. In high-pressured areas I work smaller finesse worms a lot. As for line, when rigging plastics I usually stick to fairly lightweight monofilament, from six- to twelve-pound test, on a pretty stiff baitcasting rod. You'll need a strong rod for those times when lures or fish bury themselves in the weeds, and it also helps set the hook through the plastic and into the fish.

Another prime plastic finesse approach for targeting finicky bass via spinning tackle is drop-shotting. The twist with drop-shotting is that it creates a more vertical presentation via a small hook and finesse plastic worm positioned 8 to 12 inches above a small, special ¼- to ½-ounce weight. With the weight holding the setup vertical, you can almost walk the presentation back to the boat with a semitaut line, and the plastic remains up off the bottom. Many bass anglers focus this technique in areas around steep structure like riprap or bridge pilings, and although that's an obvious place, I'll work drop-shots off breaklines, just to mix things up during a tough bite.

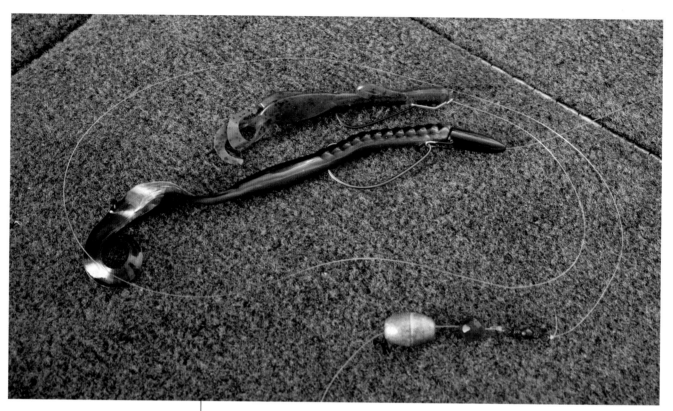

Remarkably enticing and pretty darn weedless, Texas and Carolina rigs remain among the most popular bass-fishing setups of all time. MITCH KEZAR, WINDIGOIMAGES.COM

Another option is to consider fishing your plastics rig weightless. Once, while suffering through a long, unproductive tournament day, my partner and I could see suspended fish slowly cruising around the boat, but our Texas rigs kept spooking them, despite our small (⅛-ounce) weights. Fed up and with nothing to lose, I cut off the sinker and threw the rig weightless. It worked. Within minutes, we found ourselves catching fish and back in the competition. The weightless option has been a productive part of my arsenal ever since.

When working your worm, you'll mostly want to use a classic lift-drop jigging motion. Cast it out to the edge of a weed flat, leaving enough line for it to drop—but not too much, or you'll miss the strike. Then begin pulling your rod tip to 90 degrees before letting your lure slowly drop again while taking up slack line. Repeat the process as you bring your lure back toward the boat, and monitor your line closely as that lure drops back down. (Be a line watcher!) One location hint here: Inside weed lines see significantly less pressure than outside weed lines. The water typically runs shallower, but with a little stealth you'll get some hookups.

Plastics rigging scares some people because it takes a fair amount of time on the water, mostly via trial and error, to develop the deft touch sometimes necessary to detect strikes. Hang in there, because once you figure it out, plastic worm rigging is great fun—and incredibly effective. Ask any bass angler what tool he or she couldn't live without while fishing, and you'd probably hear "plastics."

As I explained earlier, bass will lightly envelope a lure, so you may not notice a hard-core strike. Any line movement sideways, as well as a telltale, serious thump, probably signals a hit. Take up your slack line, then set the hook by swiftly pulling that rod tip back to 90 degrees. As with any fish at this point, keep your line tight and rod tip skyward. You're having fun now, but keep that fish under your control and moving toward you. Bass often live in thick cover, and you don't want that lunker to wrap itself around vegetation and get itself loose. Sometimes, especially in classic smallie water, I'll just tease bass by letting my rig play dead, then maybe I'll flick my wrist and scoot it forward a smidge. It drives those curious smallies nuts, and if I can be patient with this presentation, it produces fish!

Manufacturers sell most soft plastics in zip-lock-style bags. Store them there so that they remain pliable and don't dry out. Replace in an airtight bag properly (keeping colors separated), and you can get several uses out of a plastic worm. Though some of the newer plastic-style lures are biodegradable, many brands still are not. After several bass have pounded the life out of one, please dispose of it properly. Never throw line in the water, where it could sit for decades or choke something, like a loon.

Stickworms

Every bass tournament angler in North America keeps some fat-looking worms in their tackle box these days. The Senko-style worm looks like a long (usually 5 to 8 inches) slug, or a droopy magic marker, and the wacky rig that's evolved for their use has won a lot of tournaments this decade. Also called soft stickbaits, plastics like the Slug-Go and Fluke have a thick head and usually a narrower tail portion with an overall shapeless profile. They're not much to look at, but in the hands of a competent stick, they'll provide some enticing action because they mimic baitfish. When the chips are down, many tournament anglers turn to the soft stickbait—sometimes called a stickworm.

Hooked through the middle via a 5/0 hook, they flutter slowly to the bottom in what's called a wacky rig. (I mean literally "through the middle" so that the ends of the plastic dangle off both sides of the hook.) This technique, as I'll explain more later, has worked well for me with postspawn bass, when they often remain in a defensive, protect-the-beds mode. Taunt them with a slow-falling Senko, and they just can't resist taking an angry swipe.

If they ignore your offering on the drop, lightly twitch it back. Be forewarned—detecting these bites requires a sharp eye and sensitive touch. Watch your line (which probably is running slack) for any quiver, and monitor your rod tip closely on the pickup. If you feel any pressure, set the hook. Rather than striking this rig, they're inhaling it almost walleyelike. Nine out of 10 times, you won't feel anything until the hookset. When I first explain this to amateurs in the boat, I'll just tell them to "pick it up." If there's a fish there, great, but I don't want them wasting too much time trying to detect bites.

This weightless approach will work with other plastics, including your standard plastic worm. Just figure on using a smaller hook, say, 4/0 or 3/0. The thicker the plastic, the larger the hook or hook gap.

The wacky rig is so ridiculously simple. Via light line over clear water, this is an absolutely top technique. Know the water depth, and avoid letting the rig hit bottom—with that exposed hook, it will snag. (Weedless hooks are available and help here.) As you work it back up to the surface, shake

With a wacky rig, simply run the hook through the center of your Senko or other stickworm-style plastic. The action as this bait flutters toward the bottom drives bass nuts! MITCH KEZAR, WINDIGOIMAGES.COM

your rod tip to give the Senko some extra action. Also, know that bass have a tendency to tear wacky rigs apart. Be prepared to replace your soft stickbaits quite regularly with this technique.

Soft jerkbaits work in myriad other ways, too, from slow Texas rigging, to deadsticking, to drop-shotting, to a simple cast with a swimming retrieve. Because they're so thick and heavy, soft stickbaits can be fished weightless, which gives them an even, uniform horizontal fall fairly unique in the plastics world. They fall horizontally, and the ends flutter in a way bass can't resist. Pitch them under docks or cast them across narrow, underwater points and work them back.

Most bass anglers work soft stickbaits hard in the prespawn and postspawn period in semiweedy areas, but they'll perform the entire open-water season. Like other plastic baits, they come in every color of the rainbow, along with scented and salt-impregnated versions.

Spinnerbaits

Some old-timer tournament friends of mine lament the days before the spinnerbait hit the scene. I still remember the first time I saw someone in another boat pounding some big northern pike with a spinnerbait, then he began picking up lunker largemouths. I forget what I was using at the time, but it felt medieval compared to this bright, wiry, deadly contraption on the end of my friend's line. It seems as though aggressive presentations like spinnerbaits have lost a bit of their luster from fifteen to twenty years ago, but don't be fooled. Every bass tournament angler on the planet maintains a healthy arsenal of spinnerbaits in all shapes, colors, and sizes.

For covering water fast during an active bite, nothing else comes close to the deadly effective spinnerbait. You and a partner can fancast good-looking water with spinnerbaits that would take you many minutes with other lures. When prefishing a tournament, I've even thrown spinnerbaits without a hook. I'm not interested in lugging bass out of the water on prefishing days, so I'll confirm they're present (and build my confidence) via a few strikes on my hookless spinnerbaits, then return during the event with the real hooked deal or a finesse presentation. After testing a new location with a topwater lure (in the right conditions), spinnerbaits often are my second choice.

Unlike the plastics rig, which requires some time and failures to master, the spinnerbait is relatively idiot-proof. A hardbait, it combines a flashy

Opposite: Spinnerbaits combine a jig with one or more blades to create one of the most versatile bass presentations on the water. They're available in hundreds, maybe thousands of variations, including the tandem-bladed willow design (top), single blade, and single rounded blade. MITCH KEZAR, WINDIGOIMAGES.COM

spinner to attract bass with the versatile and effective jighead via a tough metal wire. Tie it onto the end of some tough, braided line or heavier mono on your baitcasting rod, and you can horse a spinnerbait through the thickest weeds anywhere. The wire guard connecting the hook and skirt to the spinner blade assembly forces most weeds around anything that will snag. Spinnerbaits are great starter lures for first-timers or young anglers. Though most bass anglers run spinnerbaits fairly shallow, you can fish them in virtually any type of water—from shallow to deep, from ultraclear, to heavy vegetation, to downright muddy. Windblown shorelines, where wind-created current has congregated food sources, are great places to cast spinnerbaits tipped with a scented grub. Bass have the ability to locate the noise and pulse a big spinnerbait sends through the water column, even if low visibility prevents them from seeing it.

You can alter the look of a spinnerbait in innumerable ways. The parts on spinnerbaits are interchangeable, and you can easily purchase the components and switch them out quickly. Change the color of the skirt; the length of the skirt; or the size, shape, or number of blades. Throw a buzz spin onto it, and use it as a noisy topwater lure. For more noise, attach a rattling trailer onto the hook. Vary your retrieve so that it comes bouncing enticingly past a hungry largemouth, or burn it through the water column to trigger reaction strikes.

Want it to sink faster? Add a split-shot or two to the wire in front of the jighead. Give it a completely different look by dropping the skirt and reattaching a grub or short plastic finesse worm. Put the skirt on backward, and watch the bizarre look and action that gives it. Bass fishermen and women have been mixing and matching ideas for years with spinnerbaits, and I still believe we've only scratched the surface of these versatile lures.

When purchasing spinnerbaits, you should understand the basics of blades, which come in many different styles and colors. The blade is more than a visual attractor; it also creates vibration, which bass can sense from a long way via their sensitive lateral line. (Wounded baitfish toss and twist and create herky-jerky vibration, and in most cases we want our lures to do the same thing.) Willowleaf blades have, as their name implies, a longer, narrow profile that doesn't impart as much flash or pulse to the water, but they're also less likely to hang up in thick weeds.

In general, the more turbid the water, the bigger the blade. Tandem-bladed lures add a second blade for added flash for running through murkier

water or thicker vegetation. As far as color, I generally stick with silver in clearer water and then transition to gold as the water becomes more turbid; but I keep as many different shades in my tackle box as possible. I constantly experiment and try to forget the rules! Don't be afraid to purchase spinnerbaits with some wild and crazy colors. Although I have my favorite colors, especially white and green, I've never seen a color bass didn't like, including black.

Despite all the versatility, the lure still must remain in balance. Properly tuned, a spinnerbait should run with the blades on top and the jig and skirt running underneath in strike position. Banging a spinnerbait off rocks or docks can trigger strikes, but after a while it may knock the lure out of tune. Don't worry: With a basic set of needlenose pliers and a little trial and error, it's easy to bend it back into tune. Other factors, like an ultraheavy spinner, may overwhelm the rest of the lure so that it's out of tune and ends up rotating around the spinner. Wrong idea!

The water and structure I'm fishing will partially determine the type of rod and line I employ to fish spinnerbaits. When in doubt, I usually err on the side of finesse and run lighter, but the brilliance of a spinnerbait is that you can haul it through some serious thick stuff if you support it with a stout rod and heavy line. Whatever your rod-and-reel setup, be more concerned about presenting it delicately and quietly. If a harsh plop of your spinnerbait (or any lure) spooks every fish within striking distance, there won't be any hookset to worry about. Cast it lightly underhand so that the lure lands true, then jerk your rod tip to initiate the blades.

There are many different styles of retrieves, from blazing fast to slow and steady (which allows the spinnerbait to bounce along casually), and in tournaments I'm constantly altering how I reel. With any subsurface hard lure, especially spinnerbaits and crankbaits, a popular technique is purposely slamming it against a dock post, rock, or other hard object. The idea: We're trying to get the attention of a big bass with some noise and prompt a reaction strike. You can also work a spinnerbait like a jig with the old-reliable lift-drop retrieve we mastered back in the plastics section. In deeper water, especially adjacent to a drop-off structure, the falling spinnerbait performs what we seasoned bassers call a "helicoptering" effect, which gives the lure a different look and sometimes creates strikes. Sometimes I'll do this even in shallower water, just to change the look. In addition to varying the pace of your retrieve, you should also vary the

Opposite: You can find a crankbait to work nearly any portion of the water column. Deep divers have large front lips that force the lure farther underwater as you retrieve. Topwater cranks lack the lip but entice strikes from bass watching underneath. MITCH KEZAR, WINDIGOIMAGES.COM

Opposite: Lipless crankbaits have a flat design that enables them to operate a little better in light vegetation than classic round-bodied crankbaits. To break up the monotony of using slow, finesse presentations, I will throw on a lipless crank in the spring before vegetation becomes too thick. MITCH KEZAR, WINDIGOIMAGES.COM

depth—sometimes breaking the surface, sometimes running deeper. Have fun mixing it up.

Any time fish are in aggressive mood, spinnerbaits usually are my first choice. Shallow or deep, spinnerbaits are great for covering water. Obvious times include prespawn as the water begins to warm and autumn, when bass are wearing the feedbag. Late spring and early summer, before vegetation becomes too thick, also are good times.

Crankbaits

Like spinnerbaits, crankbaits qualify as hard baits, and they're extremely popular with anglers of all skill levels. Let's face it: They're cute! They resemble the baitfish we know predators want to consume, so logic dictates that bass will chase them, right? Well, not really. Crankbaits are mostly a reaction bait that prompts a chase response in the fish. Manufacturers market these smiling, clownish-looking lures as much to people as to fish, but you can't argue with their ability to catch multiple species—from walleyes and lake trout deep into the Great White North of Canada to lunker hawgs in Alabama or California.

Even more so than a spinnerbait, a crankbait allows you to cover serious water quickly and efficiently with a lifelike lure. You can fancast it to quickly explore new water, or—although more popular with pike, walleye, and muskie anglers—troll it. (Back in my early days of fishing, I trolled a few crankbaits dangling off the back of my canoe and had great fun.) You'll see several styles in this lure category: floaters, divers, and sinkers. Most crankbaits are made from wood and plastic, and you'll find that the most effective and popular crankbaits will gobble up a sizable portion of your wallet. You can spend $5 or $6 pretty easy for quality crankbaits, so these are the most expensive lures in your tackle box. Could be worse—muskie crankbaits cost even more!

During the past couple of decades, crankbaits have exposed an entire new fish zone to savvy bass anglers for the simple reason that they've boldly gone where no hard-bodied lure has gone before—deep water. Some anglers will even jam several feet of their rod underwater to help drive their lure even deeper. The secret to a crankbait's diving ability lurks mostly in its lip, though your choice in line and retrieval speed play a role here, too. Simple physics dictates that when you retrieve fast and pull hard on the nose of a big-lipped crankbait, it will dive deep—even to 16 or 18 feet. Some new

cranks on the market dive to a precise depth quickly and then remain at that level until they rise directly at boatside. (If possible, stick to reels with low gear ratios so that lures like these remain in the strike zone longer.) Lighter line gives you more control, and it will maximize the depth of the lure. Braided lines like Fireline really cut through the water and allow the lure to dive deeply, whether you're trolling or casting. (In clear water, however, always use a fluorocarbon leader when using a braided line—for stealth purposes.)

Tuned properly, the curved bodies of crankbaits wobble in the water column as you retrieve them. As with spinnerbaits, this creates that all-important pulse or vibration that entices fish in the vicinity that probably haven't seen your crankbait. When retrieving, if you feel that natural wobble cease, you've probably got a hit. One final wobble tip I've learned from my time on the water: Smallies prefer a smaller, narrower profile with less wobble; their largie cousins like fatter cranks with a big wobble.

Since a slow, steady retrieve best allows the crank's built-in action to perform, you can pretty much forget about all those nifty retrieval ideas from the spinnerbait section. That said, occasionally I'll employ a drag-and-reel pulsing-style retrieve just to mix things up (and work different muscles in my arms.) Also, the good old stop-and-go retrieve works really well with floating crankbaits, which will rise slowly when you stop reeling, then dive deeper again when you resume your retrieve. Seems like most hits occur just after you begin reeling.

Vegetation is to crankbaits as kryptonite is to Superman, and snagging even a small hunk of weeds will destroy a crankbait's performance until you can remove it. Thanks to a pair of big treble hooks dangling on your average crankbait, they grab anything they touch; therefore, we're using them mostly in weed-free situations. That said, cast parallel to a weed line, crankbaits produce fish. And if you just can't pass on tossing a crankbait toward some vegetation, a wider lip can help divert weeds and prevent hang-ups. They're ideal in hard-bottom situations or in flooded areas around stumps or other hard structures, like rocks or docks. As I mentioned in the spinnerbait section, try bumping cranks off hard structure to prompt reaction strikes. (Whenever you're fishing a hard lure, try to cast well past the "hot spot" where you believe fish will exist.) On sandy or mucky bottoms, I'll sometimes bump the crankbait on the bottom so that it kicks up a little sediment and gets the attention of large fish. To force it into the bottom, don't be afraid to add some weight. This is one reason I'll err on the side of a longer rod (7-footers) with crankbaits. That extra length helps you direct its pathway better, as well as providing better leverage if you snag up.

Lipless crankbaits, which include artificial lures like Berkley Rattlers, probably deserve their own category, but given the name, I'll discuss them here. They're a denser, thinner profile, flat lure that you cast and retrieve just as you would traditional round crankbaits. Especially early in the season, lipless cranks perform well when ripped quickly through light vegetation. Areas with early plant growth typically warm faster because they're shallower, so baitfish and bass frequent these areas, sometimes not long after ice-out (where bass seasons are open). They're a fun, more aggressive presentation during a time of year most anglers focus on finesse, but don't expect classic hard thumps from the bass. In my experience, early spring lipless crankbait strikes feel more like an added weight. If you feel any change in tempo to your retrieve, set the hook.

Lure companies construct crankbaits in every color or color combination that you can imagine, even holographic. When I'm fishing, I usually start with natural colors like perch or shad, but you'll find some pretty funky colors and rattling cranks in my tackle box, too. If there's a downside to crankbaits, it's that large bass have become conditioned not to strike some of them. On some of the potential "world record" reservoirs of California, I'm told hard-core bass anglers devise new and unusual lures to entice fish that have seen it all. Maybe that's why larger crankbaits tend to work better in spring than summer; it's been months since the fish have seen any lures move horizontally, so they're just a little dumber.

Although some bass anglers advocate strongly for using locking snaps to quickly change lures, I generally recommend tying directly onto the crank via the Palomar knot. The less fish-spooking hardware underwater, the better; plus it maximizes the lure's vibration and performance. Ironically, if a crankbait produces quick success on a spot, I'll reject it pretty fast if a couple more casts don't produce more action. Plastics usually produce bigger fish conditioned to avoid cranks, and once I know bass are present, I want to work the area thoroughly with slower presentations.

Jigs

Jig fishing might not garner the respect it deserves among rank-and-file anglers, perhaps because they demand more focus than other presentations. Nonetheless, they're great, versatile lures, especially in cooler water situations. Imagine a spinnerbait without the wire and blades, and you understand how a jig looks. As any self-respecting North Country walleye angler knows, a jig has a heavy, lead head painted in a bright color with a single hook underneath. For bass fishing, most have a skirt (hair, rubber, plastic, or silicone) and a weed guard over the hook so that you can fish them in pretty thick cover.

Many anglers combine a skirted jig with trailer of some sort—traditionally a chunk of pork rind, hence the name "jig-and-pig," or, more often nowadays, a grub or another plastic. Good old Uncle Josh Pork adds an enticing scent factor to the jig, although scented soft baits (especially craw-shaped) like Berkley Gulp! or salt-impregnated offerings now probably tip more jigs than pork products. I think the softer feel of the trailer, especially natural pork, entices bass to hold the lure longer, giving you more time to drive home the hookset. It may not be the best lure at all times, but it's rarely a bad option, especially when targeting big bass.

If you read closely throughout this section, you know that some lures perform better than others at certain depths: crankbaits deep, tubes shallow, and spinnerbaits somewhere in between. The versatile jig can cover each of those areas, plus they'll perform in multiple cover types—from weed beds, brush piles, logs, flooded brush, reeds, lily pads, and boat docks. I also like jigs because, unlike crankbaits or other more aggressive offerings, they're more forgiving in the constantly changing weather situations we see during the spring.

Early in the season, bass tend to be shallow because of the spawn. Most males will be defending the nests, and the females that have dropped their eggs and headed for nearby deeper water, usually not far away. They'll often hold on the first piece of structure, like a breakline, or around the edges of cover, like a weed bed. You can use jigs in either situation. For shallow bass, use a lightweight jig between ⅛ and ¼ ounce, with a trailer that matches the jig size. A larger trailer will help slow the jig's fall, but attach a trailer that's too big and it won't move realistically. It's important to maintain a deft touch on your line; in more challenging conditions, say, choppy water, you'll also need to increase jig weight.

Opposite: Throw a plastic skirt on a lead-headed hook, and you've got the popular and extremely effective skirted jig presentation. Note the thick, brushlike weed guard in front of the hook, which makes the jig relatively weedless and effective in vegetation. MITCH KEZAR, WINDIGOIMAGES.COM

In deeper water, say 12 to 15 feet, the same setup will work, except you should increase the weight of the jig to between ⅜ and ½ ounce to get deeper faster. In both scenarios, I'm using a long (at least 7 feet), medium-action rod with a braided line. If I switch to smaller jigs, I may switch to a lighter setup to better detect strikes, but generally we're targeting big fish, and I don't want to lose any in the weeds. Another caveat: In ultraclear water, I may use fluorocarbon simply because the fish are less likely to see it.

From a color standpoint, I prefer green pumpkin in clear water, black in darker water, and black and blue wherever bass swim. Many colors will perform, but as a general rule the more turbid or darker the water, the darker the lure. When I fish largemouth during the late evenings, you'll often find me using a dark-colored, rubber-skirted jig. A little noise doesn't hurt either in darker or murky water, so many of my jigs have rattles hanging from the hooks.

Properly working the lure is where the rubber meets the road with jigs, and here are some high-performance retrieve styles. Just as you would with a plastic rig, cast the jig to shallow cover and hop it slowly back to the boat. You're mimicking natural forage, like crayfish or large minnows, so under clear skies and in clear water, short, slower hops look more natural. All the hook-setting rules apply here: Watch and feel your line for any side-to-side movement or any subtle differences in how it moves. (There's another reason I use braided line: It's easier to see.) When something odd occurs, set the hook!

In shallow water, try "swimming" the jig back to the boat like a spinnerbait. Bass love spinnerbaits because they mimic natural baitfish, but they see a lot of them. Give bass a different choice, and even conditioned fish might just slam your lure. Keep your rod tip up and vary your retrieve—sometimes run it smooth; other times twitch it occasionally. A growing number of tournament anglers are employing this swimming technique later in the year to target suspended postspawn fish, particularly smallies. As summer progresses, begin targeting offshore structure, such as deep weed beds or underwater point or humps, with this swimming jig technique. Of course jigs are another obvious option for flipping under docks during the heat of late summer.

In my experience, jigs sacrifice numbers of fish but improve your odds of bigger fish, especially in deep water. As I've mentioned elsewhere in these pages, here's an obvious opportunity for deadsticking. Cast it to the bottom of the breakline, and then let it sit on the bottom. Occasionally twitch or shake it a bit. Drives bass nuts!

Jigs require patience, which I freely admit could probably rank higher on my personal list of virtues, but even I take my time with jigs because they're so darn effective. No, they're not as sexy as crankbaits, but you need to include jigs in your bass-fishing arsenal. Detecting bites can frustrate beginner bass anglers, but the only way to conquer that confusion is to get out and build jigging experience. As you pulse your jig across the bottom, pay close attention to how much weight it imparts into your rod. If it suddenly feels heavier or lighter, take up your slack line and set the hook. Finally, here's an idea that may sound like sacrilege in a bassin' book: Consider spending time with a seasoned jig-fishing walleye angler. A couple days hooking those subtle-biting fish will improve your understanding of bass strikes immensely.

Topwaters

OK, I really mean it this time: Topwater lures are my favorite way to catch bass! Unlike other underwater bassin' styles, topwater presentations occur on the surface, which allows us to use three senses: sight, sound, and touch. Those exciting, classic images of a massive largemouth erupting from the calm water and engulfing a poor, defenseless fishing lure usually involve a surface presentation. Such a scene demonstrates the awesome strength of bass, and with topwater it all occurs in plain view.

Whenever you see fish surface feeding or just breaking water, that's an obvious opportunity to throw a topwater lure in their direction. Prime topwater season for me occurs postspawn, when the water temperatures are beginning to warm but remain cool compared to the heat of summer. Fish are tired and unwilling to chase a bigger, faster presentation like a spinnerbait or crankbait. They're hungry and becoming more aggressive, but the more subtle action of a topwater lure can elicit strikes. Later in summer, suspended bass in deep water will attack a popper or other topwater lure, and I'll work these lures over the shallows again in the fall. Prime hours for casting a topwater lure are early mornings and evenings over a calm, still surface. In river situations, try to find slackwater areas where the action of a topwater lure really shines.

A number of specific lures fall under the heading of topwater: poppers/chuggers, spoons and frogs, stickbaits, jerkbaits, buzzbaits, and propbaits.

As you retrieve a popper lure, its blunt front end imparts noise and a bubble trail that bass find irresistible. The herky-jerky action probably mimics a wounded fish or amphibian, which spells "easy meal" to a hungry bass. MITCH KEZAR, WINDIGOIMAGES.COM

Though different in appearance and how you'll retrieve them, most float. Buzzbaits, which look like a funky spinnerbait, are an exception to that rule. Their big blades act as little propellers to churn the water while you reel. Predatory fish see and hear their action and think "wounded baitfish on the surface!" Hauled over even the thickest weeds bed, they're great bass attractors; just make sure you keep your rod tip up and vary your retrieve as much as possible. Adding a trailer of some sort can boost the scent factor.

Stickbaits are my favorite style of topwater fishing, and a Zara Spook probably best represents the category. Saltwater and freshwater anglers alike have enjoyed great sportfishing via the simple lure, which requires you to impart action with simple starts, jerks, and pauses. When you hear the phrase "walk the dog" in bass fishing, tourney anglers usually are talking about this back-and-forth action of stickbaits. You also can deadstick, which we've mostly suggested on the bottom—except with stickbaits, it happens at the surface. Cast it out, reel a few feet, and then stop. Take a sip of coffee, check your bearings, clear out a backlash, or just do something that forces you not to twitch or touch that lure for twenty to thirty seconds. Then resume, and you'll be amazed at how often you get a strike. If you see a fish's wake behind your lure, but it won't strike, reel

How any fish can stop itself from striking a Super Spook "walked" back to the boat, I will never know. Walking the dog with a topwater stickbait is my favorite style of bass fishing. You can't beat the excitement when a massive bass envelops a topwater with a water-erupting boil. MITCH KEZAR, WINDIGOIMAGES.COM

faster. Bam, that lunker probably will strike hard. If they miss it on the first strike, slow down and keep working it; the fish may take a second or even third swipe. Stickbaits are more of a mid- to late-summer lure for me, and they deliver in open water or around structure like docks, stumps, or over weed beds. Over real clear water, I'd probably start with a stickbait, since they're the subtlest of the topwater presentations.

The difference between a hard-bodied jerkbait and a stickbait probably strikes most new anglers as pretty subtle. Jerkbaits look like slender, longer crankbaits and perform much the same way, except they're surface oriented. They're light, float, and provide us with a more subtle way to impart action on a hard-bodied lure than the traditional casting-and-wheeling style of using a crankbait. They're a great deadsticking surface lure.

Poppers or chuggers are somewhere in between the previous examples in that, like buzzbaits, they make their own noise and action, yet you can retrieve them in the same manner as a stickbait with a pause-start, pause-start cadence. Even beginner anglers have probably heard of a jitterbug—perhaps the best-known popper-style lure. Their blunt, angled heads result in an uneven retrieve that causes them to jump, or "pop," while you reel. This creates herky-jerky, noisy movement and bubbles that—again—probably mimic a wounded baitfish or amphibian. For a big bass, that spells lunch. Again, patience is a virtue; let the popper rest a bit, and wait. Fly-anglers use small poppers but follow the same retrieve principles. Hook a 3-pound smallie on a 5-weight fly rod, and you're in for a wild ride!

Propbaits, including my personal favorite, the wooden Smithwick Devil's Horse, have a funny little propeller on their nose and tail. I like to throw propbaits (and stickbaits) because it seems that bass prefer longer, thinner lures. Don't get me wrong. There are days when short, fat cranks are the only presentation that will produce, but long and thin generally has been more productive for me over the years. Prime time for propbaits occurs after the water has warmed, and every time I tie one of these, I can't help but think of the stereotypical image of a geeky propellerhead. But that's not to disrespect propbaits, which—as you retrieve them—create a churning "whoosh-whoosh" sound in the water to attract predators. You can work these torpedo-shaped lures slow or fast, but remember to allow long pauses when retrieving them. Immediately after you cast, let the ripples dissipate before reeling.

Weedless spoons and artificial frogs don't generate quite the attention from bass anglers that they did years back. Over thick lily pads (or even if allowed to sink through submerged weeds), however, both can still produce, perhaps because fewer anglers are throwing these lures anymore. A black or silver Johnson's minnow (spoon) with a chunk of pork rind skipped over the lilies sure looks enticing to me, and I usually keep a rod equipped with heavy braided line on hand for the job. A stiff metal weed guard keeps these lures fairly weedless. Pull a spoon or frog onto a big lily pad for a moment, then lightly pull it into adjacent water. That's often when the strike will occur. Like I said, I don't catch a lot of bass like this, but when I do, it's a blast.

Now let's talk a little about the hookset with surface lures. Since your first reaction when a lunker grabs for your lure is to rear back, use a medium-action rod when working topwater lures to tone that back a bit. Stay patient, and allow the bass to engulf your lure before setting the hook; but if you still drive the hook-set too early, a faster tip gives you a little room for error. Apply the same hookset rules you would with an underwater lure: Determine when to set the hook by feel, not by sight.

In the color category, I'll start fishing with perch or shad, but in a tournament situation, I keep the full color spectrum of lures available.

Topwater poses a simple line and equipment dilemma. Our gear demands some toughness, given that a big largie will head toward China (and the thickest cover in between) once he grabs our lure. That said, long casts past key structure targets are all-important, too. I use the lightest line possible—say, twelve-pound test for those lighter lures—and then play the fish high in the water column. To deliver maximum action on my topwater lures, I prefer medium- to heavy-action 7-foot rods. The thicker the slop, the heavier the action.

Early in the year, I hope for prime topwater conditions, but if these lures don't perform on a given day, I don't hesitate to switch to a spinnerbait or maybe a floating crankbait; the latter allows me to work that same slow, let-it-sit-a-few-seconds retrieve.

CHAPTER FOUR

Which Technique When

Now that we've talked technique, let's talk about which technique to use at what time during what I'd like to call "A Year in the Life of the Average Bass." Actually, we're only going to focus on the open-water season, but I think you get the picture. When the ice disappears in the middle or northern portion of the country, we bass anglers are ready to hit the water. Here are my thoughts on where we'll find bass on any given day, depending on the season.

Prespawn and Spawning

Early in the year—after ice-out in some states or around "opener" in places like my own Minnesota—I usually focus on muddy or, more appropriately, turbid bays and coves. The water has warmed faster here than in clear water, so we've got a better chance of encountering postspawn fish during the early bass season. Turbid water holds more heat, so it holds more baitfish, too. Another tip: South-facing bays will warm faster than north-facing bays. Especially early in the season, the bass aren't in the shallows strictly to spawn, although the males already are sniffing around for good bedding sites. But they're mostly hungry and following those forage sources. It's a good time for topwater presentations, especially in wind-protected bays or the leeward side of points. Early-season crappie and panfish anglers in the upper Midwest frequently bump into bass when chasing the slabs in these locations during early May, or even late April.

We're looking for a temperature in the low 60-degree range for spawning to begin. Largemouth begin spawning around 60 degrees, so I usually consider water above 63 degrees postspawn. Food takes a backseat to spawning now, though the males especially are protective of the beds and are in pretty shallow—less than 10 feet—water. Once bass begin spawning, they're pretty darn easy to catch. Generally speaking, I discourage fishing bass on the beds because it's not much of a challenge, and probably not good for the species. Pull a hovering papa bass off the bed as he tries to guard the eggs, and we risk allowing bluegills or other fish to eat the eggs. That can't be good for bass or bass fishing. If you do decide to spend a little time targeting these fish, use artificial lures to avoid gut-hooking the fish, then return them to the water quickly. Fish may venture out of the area immediately after the spawn, but I firmly believe that some big fish forage around shallow water structure year-round.

Postspawn

OK, the term "postspawn" has a certain, frankly undeserved negative connotation. If you're a parent, it's easy to imagine a lethargic mom or pop largemouth, finished with a couple weeks' worth of giving birth (laying eggs in mom's case) then defending the kids from the local punk bullies (big panfish). All they want to do is recuperate out of harm's way (the local breakline) and chill out! No eating, no fighting, no sniffing your lures, just resting. Well, it's not quite that bad, for a couple of reasons. For one, the postspawn period when females recover and males complete defending the nests only lasts about a week. For two, postspawn lethargy is overplayed; we can still catch bass at this time. They'll remain in the vicinity of the beds but hang out near that deeper-water breakline for much of the day for security, although much of their—albeit limited—feeding will occur in the shallows. Females leave the bedding area first, then the males follow a few days to a week later.

Obvious structure to target for fishing is drop-offs, inside breakline turns with rock and cabbage, points, and shallow docks adjacent to deeper depths. Always check weed edges! View these weed edges as highways from the spawning areas to deepwater summer haunts. Unique bottom structure like rock piles or sudden holes serve almost as stop signs along the way. In short, postspawn bass usually return to the same locations where we found them prior to the spawn to recover, then they'll spread out to slightly deeper water and structure.

I thoroughly fish rocky, weedy points, rock piles, and hard-bottom areas; baitfish will key on these areas. MITCH KEZAR, WINDIGOIMAGES.COM

Early Summer

Some of the best fishing of the season occurs during this time, as bass are ready to actively feed and resume the life of the freshwater piscatorial world's biggest little toughies. Everything is coming together to provide prime time for pursuing bass. They're hungry and over the postspawn blues. New plant growth has oxygenated the water nicely, and we've got an abundance of baitfish and insects emerging into the waterways. In many portions of the country, bass haven't seen an artificial lure for many months, so they're willing to slam your lures.

When working the early-summer period, monitor the bottom and weed structure as you enter the bay or cove. That milfoil or other structure at 3 to 5 feet coming off the main lake could be extremely productive. Once I'm deeper into the bay, I'll concentrate on the weed line near shore or any downed trees. Don't be afraid to key on early lily pads. They sometimes produce a fish.

As bass begin transitioning into that active, early-summer feeding phase, this is a great time for crankbaits. Also, via relatively light line in the ten- to twelve-pound-test range, use light sinkers ($\frac{1}{16}$-ounce or smaller) and a variety of plastics, such as crayfish, spider-type grubs and tubes— these are prime lures for spring bass. I've found a lot of success early in the summer with a slow-falling plastic rig for triggering strikes.

Late Summer

We have a couple of other factors working against us in late July and early August. First, the spawn ended at least a month or two earlier, and that postspawn feeding period has waned. Second, baitfish are everywhere. This isn't cold, void, unproductive early-season water. Small panfish and other baitfish have been proliferating for months and provide a steady, natural food source for predators like bass. Also, the shallows have warmed to the point that they're becoming uncomfortable to big bass under a high sun, so we're less likely to find them in those relatively easy-to-locate early-season haunts.

But we have several factors working for us. Bass are less active than they were a month ago, or will be again in early autumn, but in this warm water we've struck the heart of the growing season. Bass are feeding in midsummer, even in the shallows early and late in the day. Second, the fish may be more concentrated now than at any other time during the open-water season. During the middle portion of the day, they'll even school up off the breakline and around deeper structure. Third, because of the sometimes daunting conditions—i.e., heat and humidity—of dog days fishing, bass see less fishing pressure late in the summer than in June or early July.

For the above reasons, late-summer bass fishing usually shakes out as either really good or really bad. We can sum up location with one spot: deepwater weed lines over hard bottoms. Using your electronics, work that outside weed edge, which typically sets anywhere from 12 to 20 feet.

I'll start with crankbaits as a search tool or, if there are two people in the boat, have one person work a spinnerbait, just to mix things up. Use natural-colored cranks (remember all those new baitfish?) in perch, shad, or crawdad (crayfish) colors first.

Sometimes it takes a pass or two to learn the lay of the weed line. Watch your depthfinder to keep the boat just off the edge of the heavy weeds so that you're not wasting time clearing lures. That said, if you're pulling coontail off your lures, you're in the right place. Bass love the stuff.

Once you've nailed down the weed line location, a deep-diving crankbait works well because it gets down fast and covers a lot of water in the strike zone. Work those heavy spinnerbaits the same way, a technique bass geeks call "slow rolling." After your cast, let it settle to the bottom, give it a quick pump to activate the blades, then reel it in real slow. You're trying to keep it in the strike zone as long as possible.

Thoroughly fish weed points, rocky points, rock piles, and any hard-bottom areas. Baitfish will key on these areas, and so will the bass. Watch the surface. If you see panfish or other baitfish breaking the surface, there's a good chance a school of largemouth are feeding underneath. That's a key word here: *school*. Bass actually school up and concentrate off these deep weed lines in late summer. If you find one, you'll usually find a whole pod. After two or three strikes or releases on my search baits, I've found the school and will begin altering tactics. I'll switch to jig-and-pig or a jig and plastic. Employ a skirted jig with a weed guard, and tip it with something tasty, like a plastic trailer, salt craw, or Berkley power craw. Go ahead and try a Texas rig if you prefer—say, with a 7-inch turtleback worm or on a ⅛- to ⅜-inch jig.

When you discover a good school of bass, you can create an almost frenzied feeding (and thus fish-catching) scenario. Multiple strikes and hooked hawgs roaring to and from the boat stir up the baitfish, which in turn whip up other bass. Within seconds, you'll have the same wild-eyed grimace when you're connecting with fish every other cast.

Early Autumn

September is the second best time for fishing bass across the northern United States—after that all-important postspawn period in early June (in places like Minnesota). That statement carries an important caveat: After August fish begin to scatter, so you'll find fewer pods of largemouth. Turnover occurs in late September, and bass literally could be anywhere in the lake. Finding these fish is a challenge. Turnover occurs when layers of warm and cool water flip, usually in late September. A warm top layer that developed over the summer cools off quickly with autumn's cold evenings and eventually flips and mixes with the colder layer underneath. The mixing and chaos that occurs when the lake bottom waters rise to the top throws fish off, and pretty well trashes the bites, for upwards of a week. Once the water temperatures become consistent through midfall, bass reactivate for a great bite until really cold weather arrives. Then bass enter a cold-water lethargic funk that sends most hard-core bassers toward California or southern climes until ice-out the following spring.

But between turnover and ice, we can enjoy the great late season. The days are getting shorter, the mornings a little cooler, and bass—like their human counterparts—have the desire and energy to hunt. The harshest, strongest strikes of the year will occur during this time.

So let's tackle the challenging part of early-fall fishing equation: the search. You just read a simple rule for August bass—deep weed lines. That location and those tactics would still work if not for one little problem: The weed lines aren't there anymore. OK, that's a slight exaggeration. The weeds still exist, but some, especially the cabbage, have died back significantly by now. That means less oxygen, which is less desirable for baitfish. You know the rest by now: No baitfish, no bass.

Weeds begin greening up in May and early June in the northern United States and peak by mid-July. By late July, depending on lake clarity and bottom content, some weeds will be dying back, especially in the shallows. Bass have fewer ambush points in dying weeds, so they'll seek whatever green weeds remain. So in late summer, start there. Dig out some topwaters, watch the surface for baitfish, and cast around some heavy weed beds. Start with surface lures, then transition to jig-and-pigs. As astute readers know, I love plastics, but I find myself switching more to active lures like spinnerbaits in 8 to 10 feet of water. Remember, those wild-eyed bass are more apt to hit now because Mother Nature is telling them that winter is coming; that triggers feeding and more strikes.

When you find bass, expect quality fish in the 3- to 3½-pound range. You'll find scattered fish and fewer schools, but the quality should be pretty good. They've nearly completed an entire growing season, so they're fat and healthy. This is the time of year that state records are broken. When you find a weed pattern, it should run fairly consistent throughout the lake. A mix of green cabbage (if any still exists) and coontail is my favorite place to start.

No luck with that weed pattern? Don't give up, because here's another autumn location. Let's say things have progressed further than we first thought, and the fish are moving deeper already. In southern reservoirs, while we anglers in the North are fishing the hard water, jigging spoons are a winter bass bite lure. They'll drop them down 30 or 40 feet and jig-crank it like an ice walleye bite. Now, I'm not suggesting we employ that technique during an autumn in Minnesota or New York, but we can intercept the bass on their way to winter haunts. How? By fishing vertical, deep drops.

Deepwater breaks, especially near heavy weed flats, are one of my favorite areas in late September. Use your electronics to locate baitfish schooled on these areas. This could be over water as deep as 25 to 30 feet. Early in the day, I'll often find bass near the edge of a break, then they'll transition deeper later in the day. Toss out a jig worm with a jig, say about $^3/_{32}$ ounce. (I'm a firm believer in the lighter, the better.) Bite off half an inch of that 7-inch plastic worm, or try the same jig with a Senko. Cast it toward the break, and follow the top line back down. Even in autumn, quite often all you'll feel is extra weight when the strike occurs. Watch your line for a flick or jump, and set the hook.

Want one more, exciting option? Target the frog migration! All those amphibians are moving around and heading for the shallows to settle in for winter. Work the surviving lily-pad fields near swampy or boggy areas for bass chasing small frogs. Start with a jig-and-pig in a black-and-blue, ½- to ¾-ounce jig, with a black/blue trailer. This is a bit like dipping milfoil. You're making short casts, even pitching, not far from the boat in about 5 feet of water. Bites will be fewer and farther between using this tactic, but when they hit, you'll know it. Maybe try that black Johnson's minnow and pork frog, too.

The conditions in autumn demand versatility. Come fall, you'll find me in many lake locations chasing bass, even casting to the occasional dock if any green weeds remain in the vicinity.

It's a great time of year for catching bass. You can even sleep in a bit, since the colder water means a later bite. Yeah, they're scattered, but when you find 'em, their aggressive attitude will remind you of why we call them hawgs.

River Bass Fishing

Before moving on to destinations, I want to spend some time on a couple of exceptions to the rules. First, don't forget rivers; second, what to do in a real tough bite situation. Let's start with moving water.

Too often in the Midwest or Northeast, people dismiss rivers for bass fishing. There's the occasional smallmouth article with some fly-rod-wielding yuppie targeting those trendy bronzebacks on a scenic stream, but that's about it. Yet seasoned bass anglers know that rivers contain—pound for pound—some of the strongest largemouth bass in the country.

River fishing scares some people, and I admit that when I started, fishing big currents scared me, too. On big rivers like the Mississippi, you're dealing with lots of current, huge barges, and wing dams that can destroy your lower unit. It's intimidating to a first-timer, and you've got to be careful! Now I've fished a number of big waters, including the St. Lawrence Seaway (where there are some really huge ships), and I respect big waters instead of fearing them. In fact, I've learned to love big rivers.

Believe it or not, rivers give flatland anglers a taste of saltwater fishing sometimes 1,000 or more miles from the coast. Ever fished salt water? All those tidal forces and currents running every which way (not to mention lots of toothy predators chasing one another around) create remarkably strong, resilient fish. They're unrelenting swimmers with unbelievable endurance. River fish, like their saltwater comrades, are survivors. Burning those extra calories fighting current means river species forage more often and more aggressively than their slackwater counterparts. Bass can be tougher to pattern in rivers because of this constant foraging, but if you adjust your tactics accordingly, you'll find 'em. For starters, spend more time with active presentations like crankbaits, and place less emphasis on finesse lures like plastics.

Prime spring conditions for river-fishing bass usually start with long, gradual snowmelt and stable crests. Unlike a year with flood conditions, which scatter fish, in low-water years river largemouths are more predictable

By understanding the life cycles of bass, we can enjoy good fishing for the species during the entire open-water season. Prime times to work shallow water structure for north country largemouth (shown) typically occur in early summer or early autumn. MITCH KEZAR, WINDIGOIMAGES.COM

and easier to locate. Because the water warms faster in rivers than in lakes, river bass spawn up to a month earlier than their lake cousins. When the temperature hits 57 degrees in a river, bass start spawning. In most rivers across the northern tier of the United States, they'll wrap it up by late April or early May, whereas you're looking at June in a lot of lakes.

You'll often find smallmouth and largemouth bass in the same rivers. Follow the same rule you would on a lake: Smallies suspend more around gravel and rock, while largemouth inhabit the softer bottom areas (where there's less current). Postspawn, work vegetation and, especially early in the year, shallow, slackwater areas. We're talking 1 to 5 feet of water with a little of that precious forage-carrying current. Toss a buzzbait or spinnerbait in there, and work it back slowly and erratically.

In late May on big rivers, focus on wing dams, particularly spots where you can find a break. Occasionally a barge or towboat will bump the rocks underneath and create an opening. Largemouth bass hunker down in these breaks (commiserating with those pesky walleyes), and as the current washes minnows through, the bass gobble them up. Stay right above the breaks, and drop a tube jig. This is fun fishing!

The tough part is keeping your boat over the right spot. Spend some time studying your electronics and learning a specific wing dam top to bottom. You can also try casting spinnerbaits to shore and working them back over the wing dam. Remember, this is stained water, so flash is important. Use a No. 5 or 7 willowleaf or larger on your spinnerbait in gold or copper. If you're a late riser, you'll love river largemouth fishing. The bite seems to peak mid- to late morning, so I rarely hit the water before 8:30 or 9:00 a.m. The turbid, stained water of North Country rivers seems to mean these fish hunt best in strong daylight when they can see forage.

One of my partners a couple of years back accused me of only wanting to fish smallmouth on rivers. Upon further review: Guilty as charged. I guess the kid in me just gravitates toward those river smallies, even if it sometimes means hitting the water earlier than the average bear.

Wind plus current can equal some massive, powerful wave action. Be prepared for it, and be willing to move if it makes conditions unfishable. In a tournament with high current a few years ago, the wind and current were simply too strong. By slowly snaking my way through little channels, I found places with inlets where I felt comfortable. Obviously, be careful under such unfamiliar conditions. Once you wreck your boat, you can't fish.

But that said, I love river fishing. Again, just like salt water, you never know what you're going to catch in a river—thumping catfish, American eel, even sturgeon! And those big barges or ships I mentioned earlier? They stir up the shad, which in turn stirs up a mini feeding frenzy. And you can't beat an angry, hungry largemouth who's been fighting current all day.

Energizing a Slow Bite

Every angler—winter or summer, hard water or soft water—has experienced "the lost bite." Fish were slamming your lure yesterday, but twenty-four hours later—in identical conditions—you can't buy a strike. What's going on? First, let me assure you, such scenarios frustrate anglers of all levels, amateur and professional alike. While prefishing Lake Champlain in upstate New York/Vermont in September 2005, my co-angler and I enjoyed an absolutely fabulous smallmouth bite. Three- and 4-pounders were slamming a green-skirted spinnerbait and a chartreuse crankbait off a deep flat.

Believe it or not, my partner and I were searching for places where the fish weren't biting, just to mix up our tactics. Bottom line, it was one of the best fishing days of my life. Bet you know where this is going, right? Tournament day arrived forty-eight hours later, and the conditions looked identical: heat, dead calm, and sunny, clear skies. Yet I could not find a bite in the same locations with those two lures. The dominant thought in my head that day: They're gone!

The smallies hadn't evacuated the area. They still were there (or at least very close), but they didn't want what I was offering anymore. Here's how I salvaged the day.

One glance around the lake (many other teams were working the same flat) showed little casting occurring. Call me stubborn, but I just didn't want to adjust. Finally, I switched to a less-aggressive, tube jig presentation. Suddenly, on the same waypoints, I began catching smallies. They were in little schools, and good fishing commenced.

Two learning experiences from the day: First, being stubborn never pays off. Second, don't think just because fish aren't biting that they're not present.

In this Lake Champlain example, there was a perfectly legitimate reason the bite switched. Yeah, the conditions were identical to forty-eight hours earlier, but during the day in between, a big wind had whipped up the lake. It even kept me off the water for most of the day. Throw in several hundred hours of hard-core prefishing bassers on Champlain, and the smallies wanted a more casual dining experience! I thought the lake had settled down from the wind and pressure. It hadn't.

After the yank-your-arm-off experience of prefishing, shifting my mindset toward a more patient presentation demanded serious effort. I had no patience for a wacky- or straight-hooked worm. Slowing down wasn't easy, but it ultimately paid off. Here's a simple protocol for when you find yourself in a similar situation on local water.

Many factors can alter a hot bite: hot weather, cold fronts, big winds, no wind, fishing and boating pressure, and changing water levels. If a bite changes, take a hint from the fish, and take it quickly. First, use and trust your electronics. In the 12-foot water over this flat, we could see fish on the graph. That encouraged us to switch tactics until we found success. If they're gone, let the search commence. Start at the break—that neutral zone where stressed fish inevitably retreat.

Start slow. A simple finesse worm is my favorite—go worms for largies, tubes for smallies. A weighted jig with a nice steady fall ranks pretty high on my bassing repertoire during a tough bite. Work with your fishing partner(s) to mix it up. Maybe your buddy fancasts a search bait—a spinnerbait, rattler, or shallow-diving crank—to find active fish, while you stick with a slower presentation, like a wacky rig. Nothing doing? Work deeper. A rule of thumb: Deeper fish demand a more precise presentation, so work slowly and methodically. If nothing's happening deep, move to the shallows fast, especially early in the season.

In really shallow water (where bass anglers often find themselves), you can't see fish on screen because they're not under the boat. Throw all manner of search baits—topwater, divers, and spinners until one of you finds an active fish. Then at least one of you should revert to a slower-action lure until you find the magic bullet. Or take my advice from earlier, and pursue river-dwelling fish, which seem less susceptible to changes in weather, or whatever, affecting their behavior. Maybe it's because they cope with currents and a steadier diet of fluctuating conditions.

Sharp changes in weather aren't mandatory to shut down a bite. All these rules apply during transition times of year: spring or fall, or around the spawn. People and their attempts to improve lakes can alter the bite, too. In 2006 I enjoyed fantastic fishing on a metro area lake—we're talking a consistent catch of 3- to 5-pound fish off the weed line. Then the city or a local lake association sprayed the weed line, and the fish disappeared.

I searched and worked different spots via multiple presentations, and nothing. They didn't die, because I didn't see (or smell) rotting bass along shore, but I never did find those fish. Frankly, it bugged me all winter. Chemical spraying onshore or in the water can affect fish behavior. So can weed harvesting. Think all that milfoil cutting occurring on some lakes doesn't alter bass behavior?

Don't let a tough bite ruin your fishing. Chalk it up the challenge of fishing, then let the modern tactics and tools of twenty-first century fishing lead you to the promised bite!

CHAPTER FIVE

Bass Fishing Dilemmas ... and How I Solved Them

Let's spend a few pages solving some fishing dilemmas and quandaries that I've faced during my fifteen years of tournament fishing. Think of them as mini-mysteries involving uncooperative bass. By following the clues we've already learned and thinking outside the box, we'll put them in the boat. I've learned a lot about fishing bass from these anecdotes, and you will, too.

Double-Strikers

Once, while fishing a tournament in the Thousand Islands chain in the St. Lawrence River, I was finding success working Senkos on the inside weed lines. Working my way along, I eventually cast adjacent to a log, had a good strike and followed with a solid hookset. Somehow, however, the line broke—probably because that big fish wrapped around a branch. Now, a lot of people believe that a fish in that situation wouldn't strike again—maybe for days. Wrong!

I switched to a skirted jig-and-pig, and then flipped it to the exact same spot. Bam! When I got that 4-pound largie to the boat, my Senko was still in its mouth. That fish was hiding in there, waiting for forage to float past in an eddy's light current just off the main river. He wanted something in his face, and that combination connected. The situation reinforced a simple rule of bass fishing: If you miss a fish once, give it a whirl with something different. Bass will strike multiple times.

Lure Size Matters

Lure size can be key to catching fish, and here's an example: Early in my tournament-fishing career, I participated in an event on North South Center Lake in the Chisago Lakes region northeast of the Twin Cities. I was having a lot of luck catching 2-pound bass via a jig worm. It started out as great fun, but after catching a dozen 2-pounders, I realized my total weight was remaining static. A live well full of 2-pounders won't win many tournaments.

Then a little voice reminded me of another good bassin' rule: If you want bigger fish, try a bigger lure. There may be bigger fish among smaller ones, and they may prefer something larger. Don't get me wrong here. Large fish will take smaller lures, too, but on some days small may not be worth a big fish's time. In a school of smaller fish, try a larger lure. It worked on North South Center that day: I went from a ⅛- to a ½-ounce jigging worm and almost immediately caught two 4-pounders that put me "in the money" at that event.

I run four basic lure groups (albeit with plenty of deviations, as you've seen throughout these pages): spinnerbaits, jerkbait, topwaters, and plastic—tubes, grubs, and worms. Keep them in multiples sizes in your tackle box, from ⅛ ounce to ½ ounce, and be willing to upsize, even when you're catching fish.

Lure "Chumming"

OK, so my fishing partner Howie and I are working the smallmouth on Lake Vermillion in northeastern Minnesota. Jerkbaits were producing slow but fairly steady action in the cool water, and we realized that entire schools of smallies were following our lures back to the boat. We were getting few hits, and most hooksets involved smaller fish.

Then Howie fashioned a plan: One of us should toss a tube just past the point where the schools would back off our jerkbait. Offer them something different before they moved back to the safety of the weed line. It worked! We took turns alternating between attracting the fish with our topwaters, then hammering the big ones—cast after cast—with tube jigs. We joked that we were chumming with artificial lures, but the experience brought home an important lesson for me: Whenever possible, work together with your fishing companions, and you may both enjoy the fruits of your cooperation.

Postspawn Blues

After the spawn, when large females head for the first weed lines, bass have a reputation for being ridiculously lethargic. Two years ago, while prefishing an early-June event on Lake Minnetonka, I was swimming jigs against the inside weed line. Fish were active and biting, but twenty-four hours later—day one of the tournament—nada. The fish had finished spawning, and they were tired and lethargic.

Howie and I were marking fish and tried everything from every angle before finally hitting a successful technique. We faced the weed line from deeper water and wacky rigged. We literally had to spoon-feed those lethargic big mommas and cast from a long ways for stealth. First we thought weightless, but that wasn't working. We needed to toss it directly in the weeds, right in front of the fish, and that required a weedless hook. Lethargic yes, but they'd eat something tantalizing right in front of them. An amazingly productive day of fishing ensued, and my fishing partner and I "cashed a check." Every year since at that event (and a few others), I catch fish in there at that time. The message here: A slowly worked wacky rig is irresistible for lethargic postspawn fish.

Frog Success

Spring 2007 brought me to a chunk of water I'd never fished before: the Potomac River along Maryland, Virginia, and the Washington, D.C., area. In the Upper Midwest we have loads of milfoil, and it runs deeper than what I encountered in this East Coast waterway. Don't ask me why, but it stops at 5 to 6 feet deep in the East, whereas it runs in excess of 10 feet deep back home.

I don't fish many artificial frogs in northern climes, but I've used them extensively on the Potomac this spring and found great success in the weeds. A nifty trend has developed that's worth sharing. Over deeper water, I'm throwing bigger artificial frogs over the tops of matted weeds and getting strikes. On shallower water, fish don't like those big, noisy lures, but smaller, soft horny toads are nabbing largies. The combination of light current, shallow water, and healthy weed beds has created the successful formula, and I can't wait to employ this back home in summer.

Changing Patterns

In August 2006 on Lake Minnetonka, a fishing partner and I ran smack into a nasty weather change. Our prefishing produced lots of healthy bass in the milfoil in some high-70s-/low-80s-temperatures. The tournament starts, and sweltering mid-90s heat and bright skies arrive. Despite the weather change, we started where we found success, by flipping the foil with heavy jigs. Where we'd been catching fish like crazy the previous two days, we now found ourselves catching one here, one there at a gruelingly slow rate under that beastly sun.

Our initial thought was that the bass had moved shallower but deeper into the thick foil for protection from the direct sunlight. No dice. So we figured, if they're not on the weed edge and not shallow, they must have gone deeper. We went to the first, nearest structure we could find, some rocks at about 20 feet deep, and cast with Carolina rigs. Sitting off in deeper water, we cast to the weed edge and began retrieving. Just as we could feel it leaving the weeds, strike!

My partner switched to a bare (as opposed to skirted) football-shaped head with a crayfish-shaped, twin-tailed Yamamoto plastic. He'd let it get

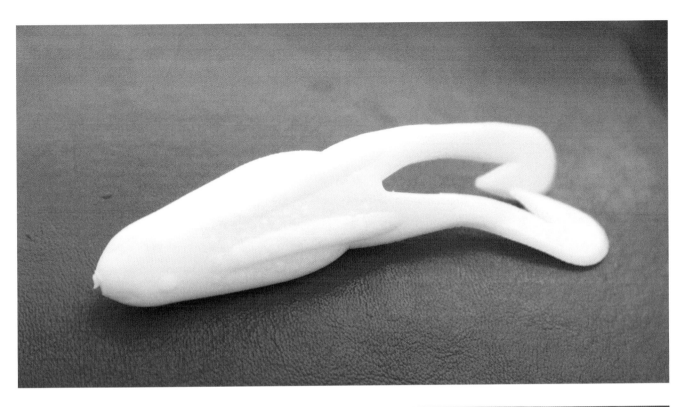

stuck for a moment in the rocks, then tease it loose to impart some killer crayfishlike action as it bounced over the rocks. Drove them nuts!

We solved this puzzle at about 11:00 a.m., and spent the remainder of the day working the pattern. Occasionally we'd try flipping the foil again, but it continued to stink, so we quickly returned to the rocks. Our final tally didn't win the tournament, but it put us in the money.

The moral of this story? He (or she) who isolates the pattern first in a tournament situation usually comes out on top. If you find fish one day, but then temperatures or conditions change, the fish aren't far away. Consider what happened here. Given the heat, my personal guess was that they went deeper. I suspect that had it been just bright sunshine, they would have headed for weeds; but it was heat and sun, so they went deeper. We had no time to search for fish somewhere else, so we went to deep spots nearby. The pattern changed, so we changed, too.

CHAPTER SIX

Fourteen Prime Bass Destinations

So, we've described all of my favorite pro tactics for fishing bass. Now the powers that be want me to tell you where to employ these techniques. I've fished hundreds of lakes and rivers, so it is with some trepidation that I've agreed to select my top 14 bass-fishing destinations across the United States and Canada. Choosing such a list has a bit of an elitist vibe to it, and that's something I've tried to avoid throughout these pages. Bass fishing belongs to Americans of all shapes, creeds, and colors: They're the common woman's fish, readily available in small lakes and ponds across the country, and that's why we love them so much. Nonetheless, I think sharing some destinations has merits on two counts.

First, if you really get into bass fishing (which I'm confident many of you will), then you may enjoy traveling to new, unusual, or otherwise interesting places to find these species. The list I'll unveil in this section contains some beautiful, historic country that's worth visiting, so even if the bass decide not to bite during your visit, you'll enjoy some fabulous scenery. Americans love to travel, so why not tow the boat and hit some of these prime bass-fishing spots while you're on the road?

The second reason is that even though many of these places may not make your list of travel destinations, I believe you still can learn from the tactics that perform there. You may recognize some of the lake or river traits I'm about to describe about these hot spots on your home water. If so, you can employ some of the same techniques and be confident that they'll perform on a waterway near you.

Like many of you, bass fishing and tournament fishing are hobbies and recreation for Karen Savik (I have a day job!), so the United States contains many excellent bass fisheries where I've never wetted a line! I'm looking forward to fishing and experiencing new water just like the readers of this book! A number of these destinations are in or near my home state of Minnesota, but that's where a good share of my fishing takes place. Again, I think the variability and learning opportunities of these lakes, rivers, and reservoirs are as important as the actual name.

Rainy Lake, Ontario, Canada

Let's start with one of the best: the Rainy Lake boundary water system on the northern border of Minnesota with Ontario. This body of water is part of a system of lakes and rivers that begin in the Boundary Waters Canoe Area Wilderness and extends through Rainy Lake, Rainy River, Lake of the Woods, and all the way up to Hudson Bay. In my experience, and in the experience of bass anglers who've been around longer than I have, Rainy Lake ranks as one of the top one or two smallmouth fisheries on Planet Earth. How's that for identifying good water?

At 345 square miles, this classic, glacially carved Canadian Shield lake qualifies as "big water" even by border country standards. In addition to smallmouth, Rainy contains a greatest hits of prime North American sportfish, including walleyes, northern pike, muskies, and lake trout. And you don't need a degree in fish biology to know that all that hard granite under the lake and exposed on its hundreds of islands is smallmouth heaven. The most difficult part about fishing Rainy's 220,000 acres is deciding where to start. Don't limit your search to the American side: The

Canadian Bass Championship occurs out of Fort Frances every year on the Maple Leaf side of Rainy Lake.

Rainy is special to me because I have friends who own a cabin on an island there. I've fished this beautiful, scenic wilderness lake many times. This is vacation country, so many rental cabins, houseboats, and other lodging options exist, too. I also will admit that it's the one waterway where I've actually eaten smallmouth. I felt terrible doing it, but hey, everyone has to try something once. Rainy is prime walleye water, so very few people are catching and eating bass here.

I've worked a lot of the 1,500 miles of shoreline on Rainy, including the Alexandria Bay area (thoroughly) many times and caught some huge smallies. There are many wonderful things about fishing Canadian water, and one is the fact that the fish seem a little dumber. When the lakes are covered by ice seven months out of the year (not to mention the relatively sparse human population of Canada), the fish simply see fewer lures—go figure. Consequently, they're more aggressive and are more likely to hit those big shiny lures that don't qualify as "finesse." Big hardware, like spinnerbaits, Mepps, and even spoons, has produced hefty bronzebacks for me on several occasions on Rainy. In a more traditional sense, you should also have tubes and grubs; bring lots of topwater lures, too. Though I've never done it, a number of guys swear by fly rods for Rainy Lake smallies, and it looks like a rip-roaring good time. Lake data from the Minnesota Department of Natural Resources showed the average smallmouth weighed in at over a pound. Battling a 4-pound smallie on a 5-weight rod while surrounded by North Country fall colors has got to be about as good as it gets for freshwater fishing. Trust me, you're in for a good time if you head to Rainy.

Lake Minnewashta, Minnesota

At 738 acres, Minnesota's Lake Minnewashta in Carver County (southwest of Minneapolis) may not strike most bassers as anything special. But this lake is near and dear to my heart for a number of reasons, partially because it's just twenty minutes from my day job and my home. I can buzz out there for a couple hours, then return for an afternoon shift. Sounds like a lake near you, too? That's the idea!

High points include decent water clarity of almost 14 feet and a sandy, mucky bottom that holds an abundance of healthy aquatic plant life. Minnesota's state record largemouth was caught in a very similar body of water nearby—Lake Auburn, in the same western Twin Cities metropolitan county. If you live in the eastern United Sates, you probably have a lake like Minnewashta near you.

When I first started fishing this lake, I worked almost exclusively a jig worm in some healthy cabbage beds. I could pull 5-pounders for hours. That was before the Eurasian water milfoil got bad; now (given the milfoil) I've switched to flipping with a jig-and-pig or Texas rig. That produces for the first half hour after locating a school, but then they just quit. You've probably been in this situation, too. I'd switch colors, then maybe pick up one more, then nothing.

A couple of my fishing buddies suggested that I get a 7-foot spinning rod with fluorocarbon leader and a good braided line, then work a ³⁄₁₆-ounce jig and worm and/or a finesse jig. So here's what I do now: When fish school after the spawn and head out to weed line for the recovery period in June, I look for turns, points, drops, and hard bottoms. Find all of them together, and you can fish all day. Later in summer, as the water heats up, I begin fishing deeper water; that's easy on Minnewashta because of the deep weed lines. There's an incognito breakline way off the eastern boat landing, and I love working the turn and tucks inside those weeds, especially if I can find a few rocks—that's my spot on a spot.

Minnewashta contains big bass, some increasingly large pike (ten years ago, the lake was notorious for hammerhandles, but that's slowly improving), and big bluegills—and it's a cute scenic little lake, to boot. Milfoil remains a problem for pleasure boaters and homeowners, although the controlled spraying for the exotic plant that occurs on the lake freaks me out more than the actual plant. Many bass anglers in North Country have simply accepted that you've got to work with the milfoil. On Minnewashta I shake a finesse jig (or a larger jig with a skirt or bit of trailer on it) a little, and the largies find it irresistible. Find those inside turns near deep water, maybe with some boulders atop a sandy bottom, and it will hold fish. Some guys call it deadsticking a lure: Just let it lie there, or barely move it. Bass can't stand it! As summer wears on, the bass will look for cover and shade. Then I spend a fair amount of time working docks or the lake's ample beds of lilies.

Sampling for bass was difficult in the past. The Minnesota Department of Natural Resources (DNR) uses gill nets and trap nets for much of its sampling, neither of which is very productive for bass, but the agency has been electrofishing Minnewashta in recent years. The results show largemouth in relatively good abundance levels and with above-average size. I can vouch for that! The average largemouth bass length was 14.2 inches; average weight was 1.7 pounds, with 15.2 percent of the bass sampled at over 18 inches. Thanks in part (or perhaps mostly) to a total catch-and-release regulation, Lake Minnewashta largies continue to sample bigger year after year.

A Carver County Regional Park provides some gorgeous green space, and that catch-and-release bass regulation on the lake keeps legions of meat anglers away. There are two public accesses on this fine lake.

Long Lake, Wisconsin

For a Minnesota girl, where the bass season usually doesn't open until Memorial Day, Wisconsin's early-May opener scratches the bassin' itch and gives me a chance to pursue some prespawn fish. At 3,300 acres, Long Lake (in northwestern Wisconsin's Washburn County) is known best as a premier walleye lake, but it also has good fishing for largemouth and smallmouth bass, northern pike, and crappies.

I have a soft spot for Long because it was the first lake that I fished as a professional angler, and I'll be honest with readers: I only caught one fish! The lake, however, has kept me coming back for more spring fishing. With its long, narrow shape (with loads of bays and other connected side lakes), Long contains an incredible amount of fine bass structure for such a relatively small body of water. From its northeast corner to its southernmost bay, Long probably doesn't stretch more than 9 miles, yet with all its twists and turns, it has nearly 100 miles of shoreline. We're in the heart of the Upper Midwest's prime walleye country here, and the DNR stocks that species extensively. But many multispecies anglers fish Long for walleyes and bass because strong, self-sustaining populations of our favorite fish live in this beautiful lake, too. A very approachable lake for new anglers, Long has many public accesses and easy-to-fish structure—plus smallies and largies in one place!

Long Lake is deep, with clear water and a lot of variety in its structure—rocky areas, sandy and gravel bars, weed beds, and a fair amount of natural woody cover. Most of the water in the lake falls within that perfect bassin' range between 5 and 20 feet. With all the wind-protected fishing locations, there are plenty of spots to fish relatively shallow bass, including around a couple of big islands. Like I said, I fish Long Lake early in the year (coldwater fishing) and have found success slowly retrieving jerkbaits for smallies. For largemouth, a jig-and-pig or a small ringworm with a little curly tail, fished slow and shallow, has produced well for me when dragging into the first breakline drop. Take your time, because these fish aren't too aggressive yet as they begin thinking spawn. I keep promising myself that I'll fish Long deeper into summer—rock piles farther out look great for postspawn smallies, and I've marked some creeks that would seem to hold largemouth later in the year, too.

As a tournament angler, I've always admired Long Lake because it's a body of water where you can win an event with big smallies or largemouth. Even in a largemouth lake in this part of the world, if there's rock, too, you're liable to find smallies. Wisconsin's Long Lake is a classic example. In most lakes containing both species, you're unlikely to find smallmouth large enough to boost your total weight into first place. On the contrary, that's very possible here, and it's a testament to the fine smallmouth fishing. With a Secchi disk reading of 12 feet, you can watch bass envelope your finesse rigs from quite a distance.

There are probably a dozen-plus Long lakes in Wisconsin (no kidding), but the one in southeastern Washburn County is in the beautiful vacation country north and slightly east of Rice Lake. Only a couple hours from the Twin Cities of Minnesota, the area offers great lodging with all the amenities.

Green Lake, Minnesota

Green Lake, in Minnesota's Kandiyohi County, has earned a reputation over the past decade as great smallmouth water. It's a lake worth highlighting here because it's an excellent bass fishery but also because it illustrates how anglers sometimes disagree over how to manage fisheries.

As part of some experimental regulations it was studying statewide, the Minnesota DNR implemented catch-and-release only for all Green Lake bass in 1997. The timing was impeccable, thanks to some strong recent year-classes of smallies. Concern about bass eating young walleyes and affecting the forage base in this 5,406-acre central Minnesota lake caused a backlash among some walleye anglers. Eventually even the DNR said that the massive increase in smallmouth probably meant less forage, which could contribute to the decrease in the number of walleyes in Green. The walleye decrease in the agency's test nets *was* dramatic, although I think the clearer waters in Green (thanks to cleaning up of local septic lines and less farm runoff) helped boost the numbers of clean-water-loving smallies and drove the light-shy walleyes to deeper water.

Nonetheless, thanks to public pressure, the bass protections have come off the lake, first in 2001, when it went to a 14-inch maximum harvest, then a 14- to 21-inch protected slot in 2003. In 2006 it reverted to a statewide six-bass limit, although at least the smallmouth season lasts only a little over three months.

Even so, thanks to the catch-and-release culture so prevalent among bass anglers, and 11.5 miles of shoreline for bass to inhabit, Green will remain an awesome bass lake for a long time. The state's record smallmouth stands at an even 8 pounds, and other than Lake Mille Lacs, Green ranks as the most mentioned water that could produce the next record. Early this decade, 6-pound smallies were not uncommon in Green. During the Minnesota DNR's last survey, in 2005, the average smallie weighed 2.2 pounds and measured almost 16 inches!

The deep (110 feet), clear lake is full of rocky structure, and some people fish them with walleyelike rigs early in the season. Live bait tends to be a bit too lethal for my taste when fishing bass, so when I fished here in the fall, I stick with jigs or tubes in green, natural pumpkin colors. Also, I love drop-shotting this lake during a warm fall, when the fish become more aggressive. (Keep in mind that in Minnesota, "warm water" is a relative term.)

Green, perhaps more than any other bass fishing destination, has taught me the importance of working the edges and sides of submerged points rather than the top. There's a big underwater point on Green where I've focused on letting my lures fall on a slack line off the steep break. Do this and you'll be amazed at how often you get bite. Aquatic vegetation is

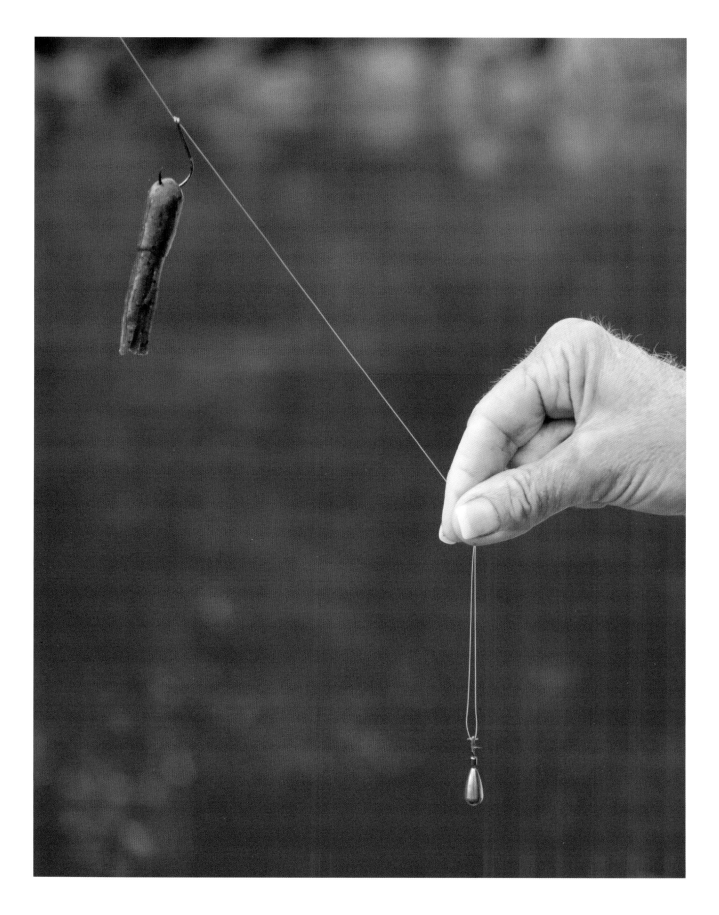

generally limited in the lake, but some Eurasian water milfoil exists. Green contains largemouth bass, but they run smaller than the bronzeback. There was, however, a big year-class of largemouth in 2002 that should be entering their bucketmouth years as the decade draws to a close.

Opposite: One of the author's favorite fall presentations on the bassy water of Minnesota's Green Lake is the drop-shot rig. For a description on how to set one up, see page 37. MITCH KEZAR, WINDIGOIMAGES.COM

West Okoboji, Iowa

Iowa's "Great Lakes" (no kidding) lie in northwestern part of the nation's top corn-producing state, and once were some of the most overlooked smallmouth water in the country. Located in Dickinson County, these glacial lakes are the largest natural lakes in the state. But Iowa for top bass fishing?

Thanks to a ton of magazine coverage during the past decade, the word is out on the fabulous bass fishing on West and East Lake Okoboji, Big Spirit, Minnewashta (Iowa), and Upper Gar. Seasoned fishing guides say these lakes rival any in North Country for consistent big smallmouth action, and if you know what you're doing, you can catch and release bronzebacks all day.

In Minnesota we sometimes joke about Iowa anglers being hard-core meat fishermen for everything, including bass. But the creel stats showing upwards of 90 percent release on Lake Okoboji don't bear that out. Like many lakes in this part of the country, there's a good profile of other "eating" fish like walleyes and panfish, so maybe that helps take pressure off bass. These are some prime, consistent smallmouth waters, and a fair number of tournaments arrive on Okoboji every year.

For the purposes of this section, I'll focus on West Okoboji—a 3,847-acre lake with a maximum depth of 136 feet. That makes it the deepest lake in Iowa and helps keep its waters cool in the middle of heartland farm country. Name the Midwestern sportfish—walleye, pike, muskie, or perch—and it probably swims in Okoboji. A piscatorial paradise, the lake produced the current Iowa record tiger muskie, northern pike, white bass, and the all-important smallmouth bass (a 7-pound, 12-ouncer in September 1990).

Thanks to a continuous bass season on most Iowa waters, I've fished Okoboji during the month of April several times. In my opinion, the smallmouth fishery is worth the hype, and it's a good largemouth lake, too. It's not an easy lake to fish, partially because of an abundance of structure, but I love a challenge!

Try fishing a tube or jig-and-pig for smallies in spring. Find any grass that you can early in the year and work it across the bottom. After the spawn, work deep water near any flats you can find on a lake map. You probably realize by now that smallies like rock points, rock piles, and reefs, and Okoboji contains all three. You can target bass via a number of presentations by working the edges of some large submerged reefs in this classic cool-water lake. Later in the year, work any rocks you mark along those deepwater transition zones. Okoboji has a reputation for small patches of weed beds that grow fairly deep—15 to 20 feet—and if you can correlate it to any rocky habitat, smallmouth love that combination.

It's also a great topwater lake, especially early or late in the open-water season, when bass are wearing the feedbag. I had an absolutely fabulous day throwing Zara Spooks one spring on Okoboji, and I've never recovered. One fabulous day like that can screw you up: It's all you ever want to cast!

Lake Vermilion, Minnesota

Lake Vermilion, in northeastern Minnesota's St. Louis County, lies within casting distance of the incredible Boundary Waters Canoe Area Wilderness and offers an unbeatable combination of scenic beauty and blue-ribbon bass water. Despite its remote setting, the 40,000-plus-acre Vermilion is very accessible and offers loads of quality lodging around the lake. With two very different basins of nearly equal size and a maximum depth of 76 feet, this North Country gem contains a variety of habitats that afford prime largemouth and smallmouth potential. Another glacially carved, Canadian Shield–type water, Lake Vermilion contains hundreds of reefs and boulder piles near drop-offs—ideal structure for smallmouth bass. Oak Narrows separates the two basins, and when I'm tournament fishing, I usually focus on one side.

The Minnesota DNR says that electrofishing catches of smallmouth bass have been relatively stable in recent years, after unusually high catches around the turn of the century. The lake produced strong year-classes of smallmouth bass in 1997, 1998, 2001, and 2002, so angling prospects for those mature age-classes are very good for the latter half of this decade. My experience suggests there are loads of smallies between 1 and 2 pounds, and a 6-pounder is more than possible.

Anglers pursuing largies usually work the shallow reeds near sandy bottom structure in the western basin. During summer, work spinnerbaits, topwater, and big crankbaits in these areas and near shorelines, even in very shallow water. Even though you're way north, Vermilion contains many shallow areas that heat up, so largies behave like their comrades farther south by taking shelter under docks, especially those adjacent to some vegetation. Unlike their southern cousins, however, they'll stay in these relatively cool shallow areas all season. Running Texas-rigged worms or tubes under docks is productive in many of the lake's bays. I've rarely fished largies on Vermilion, but when I have, those northern bays on the west side have been productive.

For smallies I've had good luck running medium-size crankbaits in natural colors over the breakline. It ranks as slightly tedious, at least until a 4-pound bronzeback bends your rod over! For smallies my boat heads first to the mouth of Pike's Bay in the southern portion (eastern basin) or Daisy Bay (west basin). In the eastern basin the islands near the town of Tower have a great reputation for producing big smallies. Don't be afraid to work docks on this side with tubes for bronzebacks, either. Later in summer, any areas where creeks or springs enter the lake and attract the cool water–loving smallmouth provide prime, fun opportunities for working topwater lures. Come fall, find rocky areas along the main lake shoreline or its dozens of islands where the water depth plunges quickly (the sheer-wall areas of border country contain a lot of these), and work deep-diving cranks. Don't be surprised if one of the lake's massive muskies (some believe it could produce Minnesota's next state record) follows or grabs your lure. Just prior to fall turnover, you'll have the time of your life working cranks or plastic grubs this way.

Finally, if you get really brave while staying in the Vermilion area, grab a canoe and try plying the waters of the nearby Boundary Waters Canoe Area Wilderness. It contains hundreds of lakes, many brimming with smallmouth that never hear the sound of a motorboat.

Mississippi River

The nation's largest river offers fine bass fishing for both species as it meanders south through the middle of the United States. Above the lock and dam system, upstream from the Twin Cities of Minneapolis/St. Paul, you'll find excellent smallmouth fishing in the free-running river. A fly-fishing-via-johnboat culture has even sprung to life there recently. For the purposes of this section, however, let's focus on the series of reservoir-like pools—compliments of the U.S. Army Corps of Engineers—that make up the Upper Mississippi from the Twin Cities to St. Louis. Millions of people live within casting distance of this great bass fishery.

This bass-lover doesn't exactly embrace heavy current with open arms, but you can't argue with the ability of current to create nifty little nooks and eddies that hold fish. A happy medium for me on the Mississippi is the slower-flow reservoir of Lake Pepin on the Minnesota-Wisconsin border. My typical smallmouth strategy focuses on notches or bulges along the shoreline—inevitably the downstream side will hold a bass or two. I cast a Carolina rig right up to the shoreline, then drag it back out. In slower current I'll even cast to the upstream side. Another technique capitalizes on the willingness of big bass to cruise the outskirts of cement culverts or bridges that abut the shoreline. Run a crankbait or virtually any rig adjacent to the cement, and it's amazing how often you'll hook a hawg.

Anywhere along the river, the fabulous wing dams hold multiple species of fish. These rocky underwater structures run at a slightly offset angle to the main Mississippi River channel to direct the bulk of the flow into the center. (As I stated earlier, in rivers—especially the Mississippi—you never know what you're going to catch!) I've had my best luck working the edges of the first or last wing dam in a series. Another good rule of thumb on the Mississippi River: Big river, smaller baits. Don't ask me why, but a smaller profile on any given lure produces more strikes for me on the Mighty Mississip'.

Now here's a contradiction for that last rule: Faster water, faster fish. You need to cover water on the Mississippi because even though the fish prefer smaller baits, they're aggressive and moving. Bass on the Mississippi River are some of the most aggressive fighting and striking fish in my part of the country. They're great fun, but don't expect to catch a whole school finesse-worming like you would in a lake scenario. In a river, everything is trying to eat everything else, so fish are on the move. You should be too.

Mississippi River bass run pretty shallow in my experience. (By the way, shore fishing opportunities abound on the Mississippi for that reason.) Along much of the upper reaches of this waterway, most anglers are pursuing walleyes or panfish, so despite the great opportunities, bass don't see much pressure beyond tournaments. Largemouth spawn in the shallow backwaters in spring, then chase forage in the thousands of minichannels between islands and other inlets off the main channel later in summer. Perhaps more so than on any other waterway, I find smallies and largies mingling on the Mississippi.

Lake Erie

Erie is the southernmost and shallowest of the Great Lakes, and although that's a poor combination for the trout and salmon many people associate with the Great Lakes, it creates a smorgasbord of bass habitat. When it comes to fishing incredibly big water like Lake Erie's 6.3 million acres, your initial search of a vast blue lakescape can be pretty daunting. Make it easy by focusing on bass habitats. When you begin eliminating unproductive, structureless water, you can hone in on obvious areas quickly.

Most of my Erie bassin' experience has occurred off the Ohio shoreline in the shallower, warmer Western Basin, which contains some of the lake's best smallmouth habitat. The islands area in the southeast corner and long, shallow reefs north of Port Clinton are especially good holding areas in spring. I've had my best luck simply drift-fishing these areas with tube baits or finesse rigs. The smallies typically have spawned by mid-May in the Western Basin (though later as you move east); postspawn they move to deep water off these spawning areas. As spring progresses to summer, the smallmouth head farther offshore to pursue forage off larger flats and reefs.

The exotic goby provides a top food source for Erie smallies, but they love crayfish, too. In summer you can mock the walleye anglers by front-trolling slowly over the edges of these offshore reefs with a tube or grub to mimic these baitfish.

Though Erie's smallmouth receive much of the press, this diverse fishery offers good largemouth fishing opportunities, too, and you can fish many of their locations just as you would on smaller bodies of water. The reefs near Port Clinton and Sandusky Bay will produce both species. Along the Pennsylvania shoreline near the city of Erie, Presque Isle Bay contains both species and calmer, flatter water for anglers who find the whole Great Lakes concept daunting. Unlike their brown cousins, who can disappear from an area quickly, the largie locations are more consistent and predictable. You can catch 2- to 4-pound largemouth all day with all the classic tactics, such as skipping Senkos or other soft baits under docks, or running spinnerbaits in the slack waters near any current—say, where a creek or culvert enters the big lake.

Since 2004 the season for all bass in the Ohio waters of Lake Erie closes from May 1 to June 29 to protect the spawning beds from nasty gobies, which will eat their eggs. Catch-and-release fishing is allowed, but do so quickly and ethically so that those bass can protect their beds and future generations of lunkers. Up the shore, in Pennsylvania and New York waters, slightly more liberal, one-over trophy regulations exist during spring spawning time. When fishing the extreme western portion of the lake, it's pretty easy to end up in Canadian waters. Make sure you know your position (some GPS chips don't include Canada structure), and be properly licensed. And expect big wind and big waves.

Anglers heading out on Lake Erie should possess a functional cell phone, a marine band radio, and commercial-grade lake maps showing reefs and other navigational hazards. Weather can change rapidly when you're fishing the tenth largest lake on Earth, and you need to be prepared to head to shore fast. Bring a healthy dose of common sense, too.

Lake Champlain, New York and Vermont

Ahhhhh, this is God's country—with a healthy dose of American history thrown in around Fort Ticonderoga and other historic sites. Though not a "great lake," so to speak, 278,000-acre (435-square-mile) Lake Champlain on the Vermont–New York (and Quebec) border contains excellent largemouth and smallmouth fisheries. Chalk that up to a variety of traits that bass love: clear water, rocky points and reefs, and abundant vegetation.

The sixth-largest lake in the United States, Champlain has more than seventy islands. At 400 feet deep, it stays cool enough for smallies (and other "cold water" species like Atlantic salmon and sturgeon), yet has plenty of shallow basins where largemouth reside. Lots of rocky islands offer fabulous structure, and a multitude of channels and current sources maintain a steady source of forage.

Other than the bays on the northeast side and South Bay on Champlain's southernmost tip, you can purchase a reciprocal fishing license that allows you fish the rest of the lake, whether it's Vermont or New York waters. In New York, all black bass fishing is strictly catch-and-release from December 1 through the second Saturday in June, and anglers must use artificial lures. Vermont also requires catch-and-release of all bass from about mid-April through early June.

I've fished both ends of Champlain and enjoyed great fishing everywhere on this lake. The southern end contains lots of milfoil, and I've caught largemouth in June by fishing tubes after the spawn. The fish had just moved out to the nearest and first weeds, which were fairly deep—say, 12 to 16 feet of water. Tournaments have brought me father north, to Plattsburgh, New York, where I've slammed the smallies via green spinnerbaits or crankbaits. Smallies on this lake also bang gold- and white-colored jerkbaits, especially in spring. Working the flats and points with these lures on windy days has been dynamite. On very windy days, mega-large Zara Spooks worked over the waves are ridiculously productive. Small ones work better on low-wind days; you can't beat topwater action like this for pure fun!

There are a couple specific places that I love on Champlain. On the north end (New York side), Windmill Point is a long, rocky finger that runs fairly shallow then dives deeper with a fair amount of grassy vegetation. Big cracks in the large underwater rocks harbor crayfish, and bass pursue them. To the right of Windmill, there's a big bay where I've found smallies roaming and swimming in schools—suspended almost like crappies. There are few weeds or other structure, so you have to search for them; but trust me, it's worth it. Like many bass havens, Champlain sees little serious pressure in the fall. Combine the gorgeous fall colors of the northeast United States with feedbag-wearing largemouth bass, and Champlain offers an impressive autumn fishery. Work late-summer and autumn smallmouth off deepwater reefs via crankbait, tubes, or grubs.

And, no, I've never seen Champy, the Loch Ness–like monster supposedly swimming Champlain's depths! Even if I had, it wouldn't keep me off this prime, beautiful chunk of bassin' water.

Thousand Islands, St. Lawrence River

The Thousand Islands region of the lower St. Lawrence River, where it borders New York and Ontario, contains excellent bass fishing and some unique international curiosities. Just like Minnesota has way more than 10,000 lakes, the Thousand Lakes Chain has way more than 1,000 islands—nearly 1,800 have some vegetation and remain above water year-round. The 50-mile chain straddles the Canada-U.S. border, and this gorgeous part of North America has been a vacation and resort destination in the Northeast for more than a century.

Let's see … loads of rocky island structure, light current carrying abundant baitfish, and cool water: Must be smallmouth country, so it's no surprise that Thousand Islands makes my top destination list (although the waterway contains healthy largemouth, too). The chain officially begins where the St. Lawrence River exits the eastern outlet of Lake Ontario, so you're near a tremendous cold-water fishery and many fine species of gamefish—from jumbo perch to muskies. There's lots of water here, and you need to focus on good structure, such as reefs and points that flare off all those islands and the shoreline, to target the bass.

This waterway contains some of the clearest water I've ever seen, partially because of—love 'em or hate 'em—zebra mussels. Viewing the bottom through such clear water 15 to 20 feet down borderline gives me vertigo, but it's remarkably beautiful. For your fishing purposes, it means these fish demand that you throw natural colors. My first mode of attack begins by throwing a weightless Senko near any island or shoal and letting it drop real slow. You'll find ample amounts of sea grass or turtle grass that holds mostly largemouth, and they must not see many wacky rigs, because they really slam this presentation during the postspawn period in June.

I've also had good luck here throwing spinnerbaits with green blades for smallmouth. In many areas you'll find patches of milfoil, and flipping these areas with a black-and-blue or green pumpkin jig has been a great second-wind technique in this waterway. You can fish the main river, where you'll obviously find more current—and more smallmouth—or work the backwater, lakelike portions. You could probably fish a lifetime for bass in the Thousand Islands region, but some prime areas that tournament anglers target include Lake of the Isles, Goose Bay, Chippewa Bay, and the Admiralty Islands. I've fished a number of tournaments here, and it's one of my favorite North Country destinations.

Many scenic little towns and a bunch of state parks border the Thousands Islands region, so it's a great place to combine a love of bass fishing with a family vacation. You can enjoy great fishing for a few hours a day, then take advantage of the scenery, sights—including some remarkable architecture—and great restaurants with your spouse or family the remainder of the day. Rental boats and charters are available if you decide not to trailer your own watercraft.

Lake St. Clair, Michigan

Sometimes forgotten, given its proximity to its Great Lake cousins, St. Clair—at 430 square miles—still qualifies as big water. A border waterway between Michigan and the Province of Ontario, Lake St. Clair provides a connection to two Great Lakes: Lake Huron to the north and Lake Erie to the south. The St. Clair River connects the lake to Lake Huron, and the Detroit River connects it to Lake Erie. An extremely shallow lake with a maximum depth of 27 feet (maintained as part of the navigation channel), St. Clair contains relatively little structure compared to most of the waterways I've outlined in this chapter.

Yet despite that lack of classic structure that we bass anglers love, St. Clair contains something else we love even more: big bass. Chalk it up to all that cold Great Lakes water recharging the oxygen levels and dumping loads of baitfish into this narrow point in the Great Lakes hourglass, but something has maintained great bass fisheries in St. Clair. It also sports trophy walleyes, muskies, and other gamefish, which is perhaps why this mini–Great Lake receives a healthy dose of fishing pressure. Michigan protects spawning bass by allowing strictly catch-and-release fishing for the species from late April through mid-June.

Maybe it's the challenge of pursuing big bass in a tough fishing situation, but I've thoroughly enjoyed the tournaments that have brought me to Lake St. Clair. Successful anglers here bring two virtues: patience and a thorough understanding of their electronics. You'll spend time driving your boat and monitoring the bottom closely for any sort of rapid depth changes, dips, inside turns, or changes in substrate content. The smallies here are on the move, and you need to hunt for them. But don't waste too much time searching: When you find a ripple of structure, drift-fish it with a tube. If that's too much like walleye fishing for you, stick to throwing spinnerbait through the ample weed beds near shore and along the shipping channel for smallies.

Largemouth probably are underfished on this lake, but you can catch some impressive ones in Anchor Bay and in the back channels by working the vegetation or skipping docks with jigs or topwater. The communities on St. Clair's eastern shore, like Grosse Pointe, are some of the most upscale in the state, so you'll see some big docks and rigs around here. Nonetheless, this is a big, highly accessible lake that deserves its inclusion here.

Beaver Lake, Arkansas

With 483 miles of shoreline, this Ozark country lake offers a veritable theme park of bass-fishing opportunities. A reservoir behind Beaver Dam, which impounds the famed White River, Beaver Lake has 31,700 acres full of smallmouth, largemouth, and spotted bass. This northeastern Arkansas reservoir lies east of Bentonville—home of Wal-Mart—and the state has loads of recreational facilities surrounding the 50-mile-long waterway. There are plenty of private facilities, like rental cottages, and guides available, too. I love fishing this lake, and my first view of Beaver Lake each spring (I usually fish it in April) is one of my favorite moments of the year.

Because it's a reservoir, Beaver Lake contains some really deep water, and the turbidity level varies dramatically, from quite clear in the upper reaches to downright dark and fertile in the lower end. Given that, you're going to work for different species in different areas of the lake. There is a seemingly endless number of inlets, creeks, and shallow structure to work in this lake, too, so don't expect to learn it all in one weekend, or even a hundred weekends!

By now you've probably realized I'm a smallie-loving gal, so I'll often begin in the northern part of lake, where the clearer water provides better smallmouth habitat, plus a few of those smaller, albeit feisty, spotted bass. These are southern black bass, and this is about as far north as I've found them, but they're great fun! I'll work the gravel bars, clay bars, big underwater rocks, and all the different kinds of rocky shorelines. The U.S. Army Corps of Engineers created the dam and Beaver Lake in the early 1960s, so you'll still find flooded timber and stumps to work with hard baits. All will hold big, beautiful smallies.

Much of Beaver Lake qualifies as "advanced water" because it doesn't contain much natural structure or cover, so you better know how to use your electronics to find fish here. Study the bottom content, and work any transitions or areas with boulders or gravel first. By the time I arrive in late spring, the fish generally are sticking to transition zones or deeper water, though I'm told that earlier in the year, the smallies can run super shallow.

As you head upstream, the reservoir widens and begins to look more like a lake. As that turbidity increases, dig out the darker lures and spinners, and begin working the largemouth. I've fished the FLW tournament series on Beaver Lake and never done super well, perhaps because I focus too much on smallies. My rule on this lake is to go light, light, light. Seems like most guys who win tournaments here do it on the spotted bass, which demand finesse. Finally, though I focus on black bass, Beaver Lake also has a tremendous reputation for its striped bass fishery. One of these days, I'll have to target those fish, too.

Kentucky Lake, Kentucky and Tennessee

Another reservoir, Kentucky Lake comes to us compliments of the Tennessee Valley Authority, which dammed the Tennessee River back in the 1940s as part of that great public works era in American history. At 160,000-plus acres (51,000 in Kentucky), it's the largest man-made lake in the eastern United States, and it's chock-full of fishing opportunities along its 2,400 miles of shoreline. The lake and surrounding public lands, including a national wildlife refuge, state and county parks, and wildlife management areas, provide one of the biggest outdoor recreation regions in this part of the country. Another reservoir, Lake Barclay—an impoundment of the Cumberland River—lies to the east; a canal connects the two, both of which extend south into Tennessee. The peninsula between the reservoirs is the famed "Land Between the Lakes" national recreational area. At 180 miles long, Kentucky Lake offers a lifetime of fishing opportunities for multiple species, including largemouth and spotted bass, plus there's enough cool water to support a smallmouth fishery. (Combined with the long growing season, this lake produces some big smallies.) It's quite simply one of the top black bass fishing destinations in the world.

Because the TVA flooded areas with homes and farms to create Kentucky Lake, there are still buildings beneath the surface. I've fished the north end of each lake, and I prefer Kentucky Lake because it runs a little clearer and therefore contains more smallmouth, especially along the eastern shore. Barclay has a reputation for being a "numbers" lake, while Kentucky Lake seems to produce larger fish. Performing well in a tournament on Kentucky can be difficult, although I've had a lot of fun trying. There are just so many places to fish, including gravel bars on the main river, downed or flooded timber, and creek arms extending in so many different directions. I'm a kid in a candy store on this body of water.

In May when I've fished the lake for largies, I'll crankbait or Carolina rig the main points, and I almost always catch fish on the downriver side of those points unless there's very little current. (Water levels will fluctuate thank to the dams.) Usually I can't focus on weeds much because of the early time of year, but as summer progresses, healthy weed beds contain spotted bass and some of the nicest, healthiest largemouth I've ever encountered. Jump from creek to creek, and work the points and weed beds along them. Later in summer, when fish stick to the cooler, deeper water of the main lake channel, anglers targeting big bass will "stroke the jig" over the grassy center ledges of that channel. That technique is simple: Pull your jig up high, hard and fast, then let it drop back down. Be prepared to use your electronics to locate cool underwater seams and channels that will contain summertime bass. Later in summer, I'm told, spotted bass will behave almost like their white bass cousins and pursue schooling shad near the surface. Toss light-colored spinnerbaits or cranks, and you may just pick up a feisty "spot" on Kentucky Lake, too.

California Bassin' Opportunities

During the past couple of decades, California has earned a reputation as the Promised Land for trophy bass fishing. Though many of my friends have raved about great days on California water, I have yet to wet a line there—although I am planning to make time soon. The state's great reputation for clear-water finesse fishing opportunities appeals to me tremendously. Do a little research on potential trophy black bass waters in the United States, and it's amazing how many California reservoirs will make a Top-10 or Top-20 list. Though neither is native to the state, largemouth and smallmouth bass first were introduced to California in the late 1800s, and the big Florida largemouth subspecies was introduced in the 1950s. The long growing season and nutrient-rich reservoir waters in this part of the country mean the fish can grow large quickly, and anyone who knows anything about bass angling expects California eventually to produce the next world-record largie.

Northern California waters have produced most trophy-size smallmouth bass in the state, while big largemouth are found in waterways statewide. California's record largemouth weighed 21 pounds, 12 ounces, and was caught in Castaic Lake (Los Angeles County) in 1991. A Pardee Reservoir fish (Calaveras County—isn't that where that jumping frog came from?) set a new smallmouth record in July 2007 with a 9-pound, 13-ounce specimen. Both of those are impressive fish, wherever you're from!

California recognizes the number of visitors to the state who have a day or two of fishing opportunity, so it offers a nifty one- or two-day license for nonresident anglers. Got a day to burn during a business trip or after a visit to Disneyland? You can hit the water for bass as a nonresident for a measly $12.10, or two days for $18.65. Check the regulations closely for season openers and closures, however. Though much of the state's black bass water is open year-round, California (to its credit) recognizes that it's got a good thing going, so it has a pretty strong system of regulations establishing special seasons and size limitations.

The state has a strong tournament scene, a vibrant bass fishing club scene, and dozens of reservoirs stocked with America's favorite sportfish plus other black bass species, like spotted bass. A long state with a steep elevation gradient, California contains some diverse fisheries—from the tidal-influenced system of the Sacramento–San Joaquin Delta, to the warm impoundments within the state's southern and northern interior, to the cooler climate (and shorter growing season) of the Shasta Cascades.

The state's reputation for big bass has become borderline ridiculous, with people expecting 10-pounders on every other cast. Wherever you go, fishing is still fishing, and you may spend hours on a California reservoir and not catching anything larger than you did "back east."

Many believe that the next world-record bass might come from two of the state's most famous bodies of water in the southern portion of the state, Castaic and Casitas. There's an old saying that you can't catch a big fish if it doesn't exist. Well, they do exist in Castaic and Casistas, although getting them to strike is another matter. Many anglers are pursuing those fish, so they're conditioned to many lures (which is one reason they've gotten so big). Those lunkers won't respond to the same-old, same-old. My friend Tim Lesmeister wrote a piece in 2007 for *Outdoor News* explaining that the more successful California anglers are modifying, customizing, or creating new lures to entice those finicky California trophies. If you're not focused on 15-plus-pounders, however, you can throw standard equipment and catch nice bass by eastern U.S. standards all day. That's a good enough reason for me to head to the Golden State!

CHAPTER SEVEN

Twenty Tips and Tricks

While I was writing this book, a number of topics and concepts felt homeless—like they really didn't fit in anywhere. What follows are several tricks, idiosyncrasies, and nuances of fishing for bass (and fishing in general) that I've boiled down into twenty tips. Some address common questions I hear from newbie anglers. Any seasoned bass-chaser probably could fill another book with aha moments and specific techniques, but these simple ones will go a long way in improving your fishing and your understanding of this great sport.

1. **Keep a logbook.** As with any hobby, you'll improve your bass fishing by maintaining a log. Just a simple notebook where you jot down the date, weather conditions, hot lures or colors, GPS coordinates, and the habitat where you located fish will suffice. After a couple of years, that notebook will serve as a treasure chest of information for specific lakes you fish frequently, success stories, or bass habits in general. Yeah, we all have great memories, but trust me, you'll remember a lot more if you write them down!

Make sure to keep your log book waterproof with a zip-lock bag so you don't risk losing any of your valuable information. MITCH KEZAR, WINDIGOIMAGES.COM

2. **Odors.** All fish have a keen sense of smell, so foul or otherwise unnatural odors may turn them off, even if they're interested in the sight or sound of your bait. Rather than holding a lure long enough for you to set the hook, a bass will spit out or release a lure that tastes or smells unnatural within a couple of seconds. For that reason, wash your hands before you go fishing with an odor-free soap, and don't mess around with the gas or the tank the same day you're fishing. (Fill up the night before.) Finally, I keep a bottle of no-scent hand soap in my boat at all times.

3. **Fish attractants.** On a related topic, I use fish-attractant sprays and gels on most of my nonscented lures and recommend you do the same, sticking with natural or forage-based scents. Another trick: When rigging with tubes, insert a piece of cotton (that you've impregnated with scent) through the bottom, and push it to the top of the tube before rigging the hook. That way, the hook will help hold the cotton and scent in place much longer than if the cotton were farther down. You can do the same thing with a truly natural scent-producer: a chunk of crawler.

4. **Fish the rain.** OK, maybe I'm biased here, since I won my first professional event fishing in the rain! Predatory fish have an

advantage over preyfish in the rain, so even though conditions may be pretty miserable above the water, bass are feeding actively under it. Because of darker skies, combined with the turbulence at the top, preyfish can't see as well, and predatory fish take advantage of this by hunting hard. As I wrote earlier, light rain (or wind) creates a mild stirring effect that scatters potential food sources and energizes the bite. But too much of a good thing, that is, very heavy rain, slows the fishing. With all the incredible new clothing specifically designed for inclement weather, there's no reason you can't be comfortable when pursuing bass in such conditions. You're also likely to encounter less competition, go figure.

5. **Water level changes.** Here's a topic that river- or reservoir-fishing anglers (and lake anglers, too) face all too often. In general, rising water levels tend to drive bass into shallower water. Baitfish may have access to fresh food sources that previously were above water, and the predatory fish are following. Newly flooded vegetation, brush, or trees offer previously unavailable habitat and forage sources, so the bass want to tear it apart. A drop in water levels will drive fish, especially big bass, into deeper water. In general, fish don't like rapid changes to their environment, so a drop in water levels means they're trying to find a consistent (cooler) habitat. As you probably can tell, if I had to choose, I'd rather fish a rising-waters situation because it almost seems to stimulate the bite.

6. **Tool kit.** For making quick adjustments to your lures, keep a handy tool kit with scissors, small needlenose pliers, a pocketknife or multiuse tool, a file, and even some quick-drying glue on hand. If your top crankbait gets knocked out of tune in your tackle box and begins running erratically, you need the pliers to quickly bend the eye (right or left) where the line attaches. During tournaments, I'll often find myself adjusting jigs in a number of ways to alter the action— trimming skirts or trailers, cutting back the weed guard, or bending the hook for short strikers. Rather than constantly replacing "supersharp" hooks, buy quality hooks that—with your file—you can sharpen regularly. A sharp hook should

Opportunities to adjust lures present themselves constantly when fishing, and a simple tool kit will make your bass fishing lifestyle so much easier and enjoyable. MITCH KEZAR, WINDIGOIMAGES.COM

hang up on your fingernail as you drag it across. Fast-drying glue gives you the option of quickly adding a bead or rattle on any number of presentations.

7. **Changes in weather.** Rapidly rising or falling barometric pressure usually throws off the bass bite for twenty-four to forty-eight hours, especially in lakes. When this occurs, I generally focus on finesse offerings such as skirted jigs tossed in heavy vegetation. Bass become lethargic during those unstable hours immediately following a cold front, and they bite about

as lightly as you can imagine—when they bite at all. Avoid shallow water areas, where the effect seems more profound, and if possible fish areas with current, like rivers. Perhaps because river bass cope with an ever-changing environment, they can better handle weather-related issues and remain on the prowl.

8. **Stealth.** Some waters run clearer than others, so you need to take steps to avoid allowing fish to see you. Casting into the wind, though more awkward, can help you avoid spooking fish. Wind creates light current that carries forage, so predatory fish—like bass—often will face into the wind. If you can cast from behind them, you're reducing the odds they'll see your boat, plus your lure will be moving in the obvious direction of natural food sources. Again, try to cast well past obvious structure, and bring the lure to them looking as realistic as possible.

9. **Chasing birds**. In late summer, black bass will school and pursue baitfish, just like their white bass cousins. Feeding bass drive shad and other preyfish to the surface where gulls and terns will join the frenzy by diving at the surface. Hence the angling phrase "chasing birds." This tactic has worked for me while fishing just about anywhere in the country, especially on reservoirs down south or the Upper Mississippi River. Bites like this usually don't last long, but you can catch a bunch of fish quickly by casting natural-looking crankbaits, Rat-L-Traps, or swimjigs that match the color. For a tournament angler, this is like winning the lottery.

10. **Night fishing.** In urban areas that feature some phenomenal bass lakes—but also a lot of loud, intense public use during the daylight hours—night fishing offers the best time frame for catching big fish. Though it defies logic, you should stick with dark-colored lures, which will silhouette better at night. I usually start with dark-colored topwater lures at night but have caught good bass on just about every type of lure during this time. Two rules: Never fish alone, and make sure your boat is properly outfitted with lights (as required by law) before venturing out.

11. **Gear ratios.** Baitcaster gear ratios vary from about 4.1 to 7.1, and they're really very simple to understand. A 7.1:1 gear ratio on a baitcaster simply means that for every one 360-degree turn of the handle, the spool holding the line spins around seven times. Bottom line: The higher the ratio, the faster you can retrieve the lure. You usually want a fast ratio for presentations like spinnerbaits or buzzbaits, but stick with a lower gear ratio with finesse lures, like plastics. An angler would have a difficult time jigging a Texas rig, for example, slow enough on a 7.1:1 baitcaster. Fast retrieves move lures out of the strike zone too quickly, so it's good to have a low-ratioed baitcaster on one of your rods.

12. **Polarized sunglasses**. Want to make a great, and mandatory, fishing investment? By a pair of quality wraparound (or partially wraparound) polarized sunglasses. They serve several purposes—most important, in protecting your eyes. Keeping your eyes covered shields your gorgeous peepers from flying hooks, lures, or big insect (especially when you're running at full throttle). Polarized glass also protects your eyes better from damaging UV sunlight, plus you'll be squinting and straining your eyes less. Oh, and did I mention that polarizing sunglasses also allow you to see deeper into the water. When you're fishing, that's a good thing. Oh, here's a tip within a tip: Wear a hat—wide brim, baseball style, whatever—to keep the sun off your head and face and reduce glare.

13. **Lure color rules.** Here's a simple rule of thumb for rule selection: Dark day, dark lure; bright day, bright lure. Darker lures silhouette better when there's less ambient light, which could highlight yellow or white lures. In dark water during overcast days, black and blue jigs work great. This even applies for topwater lures—on an overcast day, I'll use a June bug or black skirt instead of a white skirt. The second part of this rule: The clearer the water, the more natural the color. Makes sense, right? If I'm flippin' a jig in clear water, that lure better look natural simply because fish can see it very well.

14. **Spook tip.** As you've read, you've probably noticed I'm a big fan of Zara Spooks and similar topwaters. One practical

problem I've found with these lures is that they lie level in the water, and sometimes bass will miss them on the strike. To up your odds, attach an adhesive weight strip to the back so that it dips down in the water a bit. Smallies love these lures and are less likely to miss when the lure hangs down a bit. Some tournament guys are cursing that I've given this tip away, but "Power to the people," I always say!

15. **All tied up.** Don't get too bogged down in knots. There are two easy ones I use almost exclusively: the Double-Uni knot for tying leaders to my main line and the Palomar knot for tying on my lures. The superstrong Double-Uni works great for joining two lines of similar or different diameters or materials. Some say the Palomar knot leaves too much tag-end waste, but it's quick to tie with great strength, and it's easy even for beginners. Check both regularly to ensure they're tight and not fraying or weakening.

16. **Fishing Line 101.** Two quick line rules of thumb: First, always check your line, especially monofilament, for nicks or cuts; and replace it regularly. Also, avoid cheap line that retains memory. Such line won't cast as far, plus it won't allow your lure to act natural in the water. Also, line that's ridiculously heavy or ridiculously light for your lure poses problems. The former doesn't allow your lure to deliver its best action; the latter sets up a situation where a lunker fish could break your line.

Now here's my lineup, so to speak. All my spinning rods have braided line with a fluorocarbon leader. The braided line provides great sensitivity for subtle bites while finesse rigging and jigging, and the leader delivers reduced line visibility at the lure. (Braided line is less likely to tangle, a big pet peeve of mine when using spinning gear.) I change the line-test of the leader depending on the cover. In gin-clear water, such as at an event I fished during spring 2007 in Arkansas, I fished six-pound fluorocarbon while working a little jighead around trees. Yes, I risked breaking that smaller diameter line, but if you don't hook fish because your line is too obnoxious, you have no chance. My baitcasters have monofilament, and I usually start with twelve-pound test because it casts nicely, and

Opposite: Adding a red treble to the front of a crankbait adds some gill-flash realism to the lure. MITCH KEZAR, WINDIGOIMAGES .COM

that test weight allows lures to dive to adequate depths. If I want my cranks to dive deeper, I may switch to ten-pound test; if I'm casting spinnerbaits or swimming jigs in thick cover or rocks, I'll increase it to fifteen-pound test.

17. **Topwater tip**. The number one most important thing with topwater: Wait to set the hook. Don't set it until the lure is gone and you feel the strike in the handle. Then pause, take up the slack, and send your rod tip skyward. And if bass miss the lure (or you miss the hookset) on the first strike, don't stop reeling. Keep the lure moving. Give Billy Bass an opportunity to study a stationary artificial lure, and he may decide not to strike again.

18. **Red hooks.** Some anglers swear by red hooks 24/7, believing they simulate the red gill or blood on a wounded baitfish. Though I'll occasionally use them on drop-shot rigs, I mostly use red trebles on my crankbaits' front hook. Crankbaits are running fast, and a lot of pros believe that red up front mimics a gill flash. Try them, especially on fast-swimming crankbaits. One caveat: Any time you change hooks on a lure, cast it out for a test run to double-check the action. Hooks significantly lighter or heavier than appropriate for a lure, especially cranks, can disrupt its wobble.

19. **Marker buoys.** It's easy to drift away and lose your bearings, so when you catch a bass while search-fishing, toss out a marker buoy. To avoid working too much marginal bass habitat, I'll sometimes drift a point without casting and drop two buoys— one over a good-looking inside turn and another where the point ends (a natural crossroads with lots of fish movement). Then I'll target those two spots fast and dirty. Deep water, where there are few natural lakeshore objects to align your location, is a logical place to drop a marker buoy. When you catch a fish in weeds, sometimes torn-up, floating vegetation can serve as a natural marker buoy if you want to be discreet and not alert other anglers to your spot.

20. **Landing bass.** Neither smallmouth nor largemouth bass have teeth, so many regular bass anglers "lip" their bass by hand when landing them. Paying attention to the hook(s) on your

lure, you simply pinch the lower jaw between your thumb and index finger, then lift. This temporarily paralyzes all bass and gives you the opportunity for a quick photo and release or a safe deposit in a live well. With really big fish, their body weight can put a lot of pressure on them during lipping, so you may want to place one hand under your catch's belly. I avoid nets when fishing for fun because anything that touches a fish's body can remove its important slime layer and decrease its chances of survival after release. Try to handle them with wet hands.

A quick release will ensure that future generations of anglers can enjoy the same quality of bass fishing that we can take for granted today. MITCH KEZAR, WINDIGOIMAGES.COM

CHAPTER EIGHT

Building the Next Generation of Bassers

During 2007 as the U.S. Fish and Wildlife Service released its state-by-state reports on hunting and fishing trends, we saw some sobering headlines. The number of people participating in these sports continues to show a gradual decline, and among young people—especially tweeners and young adults—we're seeing growing disinterest in the natural world.

As the parent of two young women, I can partially understand how that's happened. Kids have so many outlets these days that I never dreamed about as a youngster. Plasma TVs, hundreds of cable channels, the Internet, Xboxes, year-round sports, music, dance—all that's just the tip of the iceberg. Throw in the growing access problems for modern hunters, and it's easy to see why the shooting sports are suffering the loss in participants. But you know what, folks? Fishing doesn't have that problem. The water in America belongs to all people, and it's rarely inaccessible to anyone.

Nonetheless, the decline in the numbers of young people heading out of doors is scary for many reasons. It troubles me because, as I said in the introduction, I want to share the wonderful world of fishing with

more people. Fishing license fees and the excise taxes we pay on fishing equipment fund a good share of the stocking programs and fish habitat improvement that occurs all across the country. Even people who never step outside benefit from these expenditures, via a healthier environment. But if the next generation doesn't step up and become active in the fishing sports, who's going to fund all that? Where will the next generation of tournament pros come from?

There's an answer and it involves each of us taking the time to introduce a kid to fishing. Many of us have encountered those situations where we're planning a multi-hour trip with children, and after fifteen minutes, the kid or kids are whining: "We're bored! We want to go home!" Wrong approach, obviously.

So how do we keep kids interested in what we're doing so they remain participants for life? Well, I can't promise that, but I can throw out some ideas that should at least keep them from driving you, their loving mentor, nuts for a couple of hours.

Fishing with Kids Do's and Don'ts

Do bring live bait. Normally, I'm not a big fan of using live bait, especially for bass, but when fishing with young kids, I make an exception. Fish are more likely to gut-hook themselves with live bait, and that makes successful catch-and-release more difficult, because that fish is just less likely to survive. But the simple fact is that you're going to get more action using live bait, and action is what kids demand.

When the fish aren't biting, some curious little kids can occupy themselves for hours by poking and prodding the minnow bucket or worm container. As adults, our gut instinct is to bark, "Get out of there!" but avoid that temptation. Explain what you're using for live bait, why it's effective, and where the bait came from. Kids ask questions you probably won't know the answers to yourself, but by discovering responses for them, you might just become a better angler yourself.

Do mix it up. I remember sitting in on one of my daughter's kindergarten or preschool classes years ago. Besides being utterly amazed at the patience those teachers displayed, I noticed a method to their madness. They rarely focused on any one task for more than twenty minutes before switching to something new. Kids by their nature have short attention spans, and—I don't care if you're a former Marine Corps drill instructor—we're never going to change that, so don't try. Teachers understand that fact, and we should, too. So instead of taking a kid backtrolling for walleyes for hours, work on mixing up your tactics. Bobber fish for a little while. Bass aren't shy about taking the occasional worm on a hook. Then try casting a crankbait or spinnerbait. That not working? Show them how to wacky rig or drag a Texas Rig across the bottom. These aren't difficult techniques for 8- or 9-year-olds.

While you're helping them with their technique, keep your line in the water, too, so you can maximize the potential for fish. Keep it simple and do something low maintenance like placing a big sucker minnow under a bobber and letting it sit. You can focus on the kids, not your line, and if something takes your minnow—maybe a bass or larger pike—you and your young companion will have lots of fun playing the fish.

I know this is a bass fishing book, but kids don't care what they catch. Think about that before you head out. Those lake reports I suggested that you use as research tools? Use them now to ensure you're taking kids to a lake with multiple species of fish. They love variety, so don't take them to some mudhole filled with nothing but carp and bullhead. (That's not to diss roughfish, which can put up an awesome fight. Kids don't care what they're catching, so be upbeat no matter what's biting, even if it is an ugly carp.)

Consider which species you're targeting and how you're targeting it. One parent lamented to me that his kid was really crabby after two hours of trolling for lake trout from a canoe. Let's see, trolling for two hours in a canoe with no bites. I'm not sure I could handle that! They call muskies the "fish of 10,000 casts," so that's probably not the species to target with a new angler, either, eh?

Every list of kid fishing recommendations suggests working the bluegills and sunnies. That's a great place to start, however, everyone— doesn't matter what the age—gets sick of catching 3-inch bluegills after thirty minutes. I can think of no species that offers a more logical next step than the bountiful bass we've described in this book! Kids love the word "bass"!

Do be willing to move. Not only should you be prepared to change the species you're targeting, but if possible, change fishing spots frequently, too.

I've had some fishing trips (with adult newbies and kids alike) transform into boat tours, and that's OK, because everyone likes seeing new places.

Don't discount the brainpower of a little kid. Talk a lot about the species of fish you're pursuing while they're fishing. I know a 5-year-old who almost drives his parents nuts talking about fish, and he can recite some facts about "salmonids" and "the bass family" (no kidding) that many adult fishermen don't know.

While fishing, engage their brains in ways beyond constant physical stimulation. When you're switching lures or rods, explain why you're doing it. They may not absorb every fact you throw out during conversation, but even if a small percentage of it sticks, you're that much closer to building a fishing partner for life.

Do focus on the child. Another fishing (or hunting) rule when out-of-doors with youngsters: Make the child the focus of the attention. I've seen too many parents focusing on themselves and their recreational success. If that's your goal, more power to you, but leave the kids at home. Both of you are going to end up frustrated and angry if you're focused on yourself and not the high-maintenance-by-nature kid. This is their time to ask 1.2 billion questions and be ridiculously persistent without you becoming impatient.

Do pre-rig as much of your tackle as possible before hitting the water. The less downtime with kids, the better.

Do bring food, lots of it. Yes, I know there's an obesity problem in America, so bring a cooler with healthful snacks, like raisins, fruit, kiddie sandwiches, yogurt, whatever. When the whining pushes you to your breaking point, give them some food. It might just calm them down until the fishing action picks up.

Do keep trips short and sweet by choosing nearby waterways for your initial trips. Nothing's worse than crabby kids already worn out from an epic drive before you even wet a line. Mom-and-pop family-oriented resorts (which sadly are becoming harder to find) are great places to expose kids to fishing. Help them the first time or two to get set up, then let them do it themselves and learn from their own mistakes.

Don't go out-of-doors unprepared. Take it from a gal who's spent thousands of hours recreating on the water: The outdoors can be pretty unforgiving. Try to choose weather and an all-around environment that will provide youngsters with a good experience. You can help by setting off well-prepared with lots of sunscreen, bug dope, and functional clothing starting with a good cap.

Do use decent equipment. Many people recommend using spincast equipment for kids. That's fine, though I've had as much luck using spinning reels with kids. My only advice here would be to purchase mid-quality equipment (and line) that's less prone to tangles and hang-ups.

You'll fuel the anticipation if the child has his or her own equipment. It just puts a little more ownership into the whole experience. That said, I recognize that not every child or parent can afford decent equipment, but here's some advice I offered some low-income kids and parents at a children's seminar I gave last year: Take a couple kids to a boat landing with a nearby fishing pier or dock where you can fish. (Such spots usually have portable toilets, which the kids will appreciate.) Have the kids bring a five-gallon bucket with a sponge or two and load them down with drinks and sweets. Throw a bag of ice on top if needed. As boats leave the lake, the kids can ask if the owner would be willing to part with a couple bucks to have their boats scrubbed down. (In Minnesota, we're required to scrutinize our boats when they come off the lake to ensure that we're not transporting Eurasian water milfoil.)

Take it from a professional angler who's scrubbed down more than her fair share of boats over the years: I'd love to pay a couple of hard-working kids $5 to give my boat a quick once-over now and then. On a busy weekend day, a kid could make more than enough to buy him- or herself a fine rod-and-reel combo to enjoy many years of fishing.

At the end of the day, make sure the kids pick up all their trash, and encourage youngsters to leave the out-of-doors better than they found it. Throw the trash in that bucket, and toss it all out in the proper receptacle on your way home.

As for tackle, simple lures to keep in their own tackle box include beetle spins, crankbaits, spinnerbaits, and a Senko. That latter is super easy to wacky rig, and it will clean up on bass of all sizes. With hardbaits, kids will cast their brains out, so buy some inexpensive styles in case they get snagged and break off.

Do be safe. It should go without saying, but it bears repeating: Make sure the kids are wearing their life jackets, and set a good example by wearing yours, too.

Very few people in the Lower 48 don't live within a few minutes, or at most a couple of hours, of a waterway that can produce bass like this. MITCH KEZAR, WINDIGOIMAGES.COM

Do practice conservation. In my experience, kids take to catch-and-release better than most older folks. They love to watch a fish disappear with a flick of its tail and the promise to be caught again another day. If you catch bass, show kids how to lip them, and snap pictures quickly. Explain that a fish is holding its breath whenever it's not in the water.

Do keep some small fish to eat. Keeping a few bluegills and sunnies, then step-by-step cleaning and cooking the fish is a process kids enjoy and gives them a better understanding and respect for the fish and their food in general. And it's like the old saying, "Teach a person to fish, and he'll never go hungry!"

Finally, if you're an adult and personally disinterested in fishing, look into any programs your state natural resources agency may have for exposing youth to fishing. My home state, Minnesota, has the MinnAqua program that has introduced thousands of kids to safe, affordable, and successful fishing via fun clinics at easy-to-access water.

My kids still fish with me and a highlight of my tournament career was the time my daughter Britta partnered an event with me and caught the most fish in our boat!

I'll leave you with this story. A professional angling friend of mine wanted desperately for his son to join him as an amateur angler on a pro tour. The kid took to the competition and all-day fishing like a postspawn bass to a breakline. Now my friend complains that he doesn't fish enough anymore because his son is constantly "borrowing" his boat!

Be careful teaching kids to fish: You might just create an angling monster! What a great problem to have.

CHAPTER NINE

Pretournament Research

Professional bass anglers on just about every tour, be it BASS or FLW, invest some time before each tournament researching the water they will be fishing. Unless you've been on the tour for twenty-five years and have fished a lake fifty-six times in every season under every condition possible, pretournament research is a big key to winning, or at least cashing a check. Well before the tackle is organized, baits are checked, boats are readied, and the trucks are loaded, top

Jimmy Mason does the unglamorous but important work of checking and organizing baits before a tournament. DAVID DIRKS

Make sure you have all the gear you want to bring with you before you leave for a tournament. DAVID DIRKS

bass professionals are doing their homework. It's not glamorous, but it's part of the business.

The investment of time into pretournament research has many benefits. Key among them:

- It gives you a chance to become familiar with a body of water well before you arrive, which saves you time and money. Knowing what gear to bring and what kinds of conditions you'll find in that season improves your ability to keep yourself organized.
- You'll discover what you didn't know about the water. The more you peel that lake or river back, the more you realize you need to know about it.
- Researching a body of water and answering critical questions about its character will open up more questions. By asking more questions, you'll gain a perspective about the water and how you can prepare and fish it successfully.
- Research helps you eliminate unproductive water. Some tournaments are held on gigantic bodies of water. There isn't enough time to check the entire lake, so research can help you eliminate unproductive areas sooner. This leaves you with a better setup for your practice time.
- Pretournament research will put you competitively ahead of anglers who didn't bother to spend the time. You'll

already have a huge advantage over those who think their skills and experience will be enough to lead them to victory.

SOME KEY QUESTIONS TO ASK ABOUT A BODY OF WATER AS YOU CONDUCT YOUR RESEARCH

- What parts of the lake seem to be producing in recent tournaments?
- What kinds of vegetation are available and where are they located?
- At what depths are the fish suspended?
- What are the water temperatures of the lake in the season?
- What is the water clarity?
- What is the water level of the lake?
- What kinds of lure trends have won the tournament? What was the bait that won the tournament?
- What has been the weather pattern in the area very recently?
- What is the weather forecast for the next several weeks?
- What weight of fish has it taken to win a tournament recently?
- What have been the average daily weights of fish on this lake?

Researching Maps

No self-respecting, successful tournament angler goes to a competitive event without reviewing either an electronic or paper map of the lake or river. Most tournament victories are built on the foundation of a well-worn, marked-up map. It's a tool that can help you figure out where you don't want to fish during practice, and a well-annotated map can help you find potential spots for bass when your practice has not gone well. If you capture enough information with it, it becomes the living history of a body of water. Seasonal influences, special situations, drawings of structure not printed on the map, and other nuances of the water and the fish can be noted for current and future tournaments.

Frank Scalish: "My favorite thing is a map. A good map will tell you a lot. Today, with [electronics], you have tools that weren't even dreamed of when I first started fishing. I'm a structure fisherman by love and addiction, and if I found rock piles, I used to remember them by cross-triangulation. I had notebooks and notebooks of information on lakes. Maps are important but not always accurate. They

The lake maps available today are full of detailed information about the water. Adding your own notes provides a rich database of tournament information.
DAVID DIRKS

can give you a basic idea of where to look.

"I'll have five or six maps for each lake. I was fishing Lake Hartwell years ago and had never fished it before. It was a Jerry Rind tournament. I'd catch a few fish and then not catch anything for a while. This repeated itself all during the day. Armed with my map and GPS, I discovered that every time I was catching a fish, the pattern was inside channel bends and riprap. The next day I went from catching fish every now and then to catching them all day long. It was an incredible pattern."

Jimmy Mason: "The first thing I do at the beginning of the [tournament] year is order all the maps for each lake. I like to order different maps for the same lake because there are times when you'll see something on one map that will not be on the others, so it's good to see a variety of maps.

"If I'm fishing a TVA [Tennessee Valley Authority] or Army Corps of Engineers lake, I'll order a set of the government maps. They are some of the most detailed.

The TVA maps are some of the best for those TVA lakes. I'll usually end up with two or three maps per lake.

"Using maps allows me to get the big picture of how far everything is apart on the lake. If you're looking at, say, secondary points on a creek, you can look around and get a bigger view of other creeks that might have similar points."

Terry Scroggins: For Scroggins, there's a world of difference between the pretournament research he did when he started competitive bass fishing and now: "Once you go to all these reservoirs, lakes, and rivers four or five times each, you start to learn them."

While he had used hard-copy maps and other such tools in the early part of his career, he now relies on his Navionics package for the lake research he does before and during a tournament. "I use Lowrance electronics and the Navionics chips. With their mapping ability, it's like a 'live' map of the water. I really, really rely on that more than anything. . . . Once I

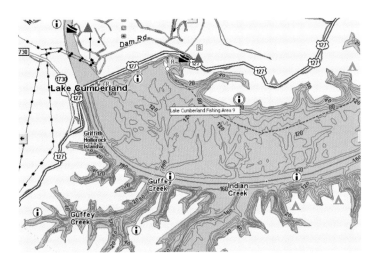

Electronic lake maps have extraordinary detail, and almost every pro uses them today.
DAVID DIRKS

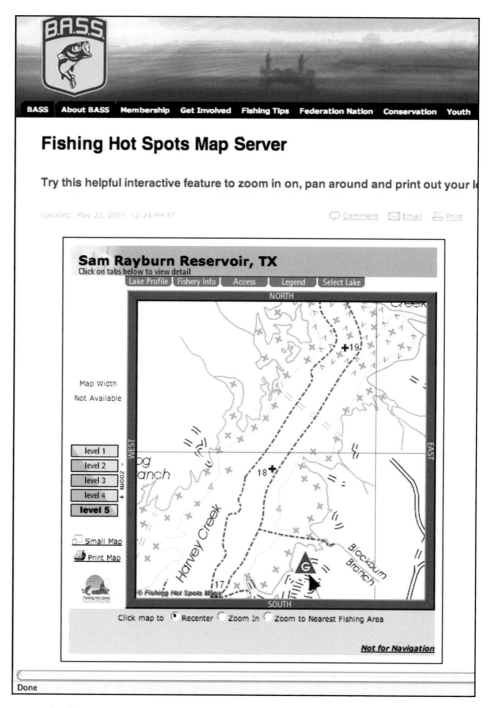

Example of a free Internet map. DAVID DIRKS

leave home [for a tournament], I use my Navionics chip because it's so detailed. I know it sounds really simple, but it's showing you everything you need to know as you're driving across the lake."

Scroggins views the technology and mapping as only a way to get started and not enough to win a tournament. Given that most everyone on the tournament trail has access to electronic mapping software these days, it takes more than good mapping skills to win.

Internet Research

The World Wide Web has brought an explosion of information on bass, recreational bass fishing, and competitive bass fishing. While there are literally thousands of books available on bass fishing and many fine bass magazines, the Internet has created a deep well of information and data from a vast number of recreational anglers, tournament anglers, and a multitude of bass-related companies. A search on the Web for "tournament bass fishing" brings up 381,000 results, and "bass fishing" alone results in a whopping 6,550,000 results. Enter "Terry Scroggins" and you get 86,500 results. Want more information on Lake Amistad? That will net you about 48,700 results. You get the picture.

Will you sort through 6,550,000 results, or even 48,700? Of course you aren't. If your search results are in the millions, your search is too broad. Here are some ways to sharpen your search and narrow it down to the most useful results:

- Use more than one word. One-word queries are just too broad for an Internet search.
- Drop common words like "the" and "it." Stick to your search target.
- If you're searching a specific phrase, put it in quotes. Typing "Terry Scroggins" inside quotation marks yields 6,010 results instead of 48,700.
- Use all lowercase letters to save time. There is no need to capitalize.

Scalish: Like many top pros, Scalish uses the Internet for pretournament research and recommends looking for recent local tournaments held on the lake you are going to fish. "I try to look for tournaments that have at least twenty-five to thirty boats because those are generally local tournaments. And then I look for tournaments with two hundred boats or more."

Scalish is looking for the "spread of weight" in those tournaments. "The most important thing to ask yourself is, what kinds of weights is this lake producing? Am I going to be OK catching 2-pounders, or do I need to catch 4-pounders? Is 10 pounds of weight per day good on this lake, or do I need 15? If you know the lake is capable of producing 11 pounds per day and you're catching 16 pounds during practice, you know you're going to be sitting in the top ten when it's all said and done."

Sam Swett combines both paper maps and Google Earth mapping to find potential hot spots during his research. SAM SWETT

While preparing for an upcoming tournament on Falcon Lake in Texas, Scalish found a previous tournament that was held about the same time as the one he was preparing for. "I found that they had 280 boats in this tournament, so I looked at how far down the list 20 pounds of weight went and found out that seventy-fifth place was 20.9 pounds and seventy-sixth place was 19.12 pounds. That tells me that 20 pounds a day is not going to give me a $10,000 check. By looking at that information, if I want to be in the top ten, I'm going to need 30

pounds of fish per day. I'll need 23 pounds per day just to make money. The winner of the previous tournament on Falcon Lake had nearly 50 pounds of fish per day! This is a spring tournament, so the weights were appropriate for that time of year."

Sam Swett: Swett uses Google Earth satellite imagery to show him a lot more of the lake than a paper map. With his paper map open in front of the computer screen, Swett will compare areas of the lake to what the satellite image shows. He may be able to see such areas as flooded trees or

Frank Scalish sets the hook on another quality fish during practice time. LURENET.COM

stumps and draw those onto his map. "I'm also looking at the lake levels. Is the lake flooded? How high is it flooded? I try to study the shoreline. Does it have timber that is flooded? Can I get my boat into the flooded farm pond near the lake? I'll put a question mark on the map if I'm not sure of the lake terrain and should verify it during practice. If for some reason I don't get the chance to pre-fish the lake, this process saves a lot of time."

If there is a lack of recent reports on a specific lake, Swett will look for Internet-based reports on similar lakes nearby. It can give him hints as to what the bass are doing from a regional perspective.

Randy Howell: "Sometimes using the Internet, I can call someone with a fishing report whose name I've gotten off of a Web site and shoot the bull about what the lake looks like, what the water level is, and what typical patterns will be used during the season. I'll get most of the information that I want myself that way." He acknowledges that you still need to find your own fish and places to fish for them. "Finding

Being able to fish in all kinds of cover and under all weather conditions is key to tournament success. DAVID DIRKS

your own fish and using your own [fishing] strengths and ability will always pay more dividends than just getting a marked map from somebody and trying to fish somebody else's holes. It's knowing how to use information that you get that is the key more than anything else."

Howell also pays close attention to previous catch weights in recent tournaments. "That gives us an accurate read on what kinds of weights you'll need to catch to be competitive. With a thirty-day off-limits, where we can't talk to anybody

anyway, I'm relying on what I read on the Internet for tournament results."

In addition, Howell will try to find out where the predominant release area is on the lake or river. "Those areas are heavily stocked, weekend after weekend. That bass release area especially comes into play when you know there's been, say, a thousand bass let go in the past six weeks. Whether they stay in the boat ramp area or not, they're going to move around but not go more than 5 miles [from the release area]. To effectively fish those release areas, be sure to fish the boat ramp areas, the rip-rap leading up to the release areas, and the docks near the release area."

Seasonal Patterns and Weather

Bass are creatures of seasons. Their seasonal habits are well-known and have been documented in detail in countless bass books and magazines. Each season has its own special behavioral impact on bass. Springtime and early summer bring them up shallow to spawn, and fall and winter conspire to bring them back into the deep. While bass might be creatures of seasonal influence, that doesn't guarantee you anything. Seasonal patterns only give you a good starting point for building your fishing practice plan.

The greatest variable of all in tournament bass fishing is the weather, and it is also the variable that is well outside the control of any angler. It's entirely unpredictable at times, and the only sure thing is what the weather was yesterday. However, paying close attention to weather patterns within each season will help you become more effective at solving fishing problems and making good decisions.

Scalish: "The key is understanding seasonal patterns. You have to know what season it is in the place you're going to fish. Spring in Florida is winter in the Northeast. With an understanding of what seasonal pattern the lake you're going to fish is in and a map, you can eliminate three-quarters of the water available to fish [during a tournament]. The bass have to be in certain places dictated by the season. If you know it's spring, you know the fish are going to be near or at spawn. Looking at your map and studying the lake contour lines, you need to find the biggest flats on the lake. You'll need to concentrate on areas where the depth is 0 to 5 feet or 0 to 10 feet."

Scalish looks at the last three weeks of weather leading into the tournament. "I just want to see what the trends are. As for weather during a tournament, it's going to be what it's going to be. I don't worry too much about weather during a tournament."

Weather patterns in one area of the country versus another can sometimes have a different effect on the bass, Scalish notes. "In Florida, when a cold front hits, it's the worst thing that could ever happen to you. The bite in Florida goes to nothing in cold-front situations, but it's only in Florida that this seems to hold true. Where I live [near the Great Lakes], cold fronts don't mess the fish up. We have so many cold fronts that if the fish stopped eating every time one came in, they'd starve to death."

Mason: "One thing I do to learn the specific traits of a particular body of water is to review every *Bass Times* and *Bassmaster* magazine I have that relates to that specific water. I also have a good database of information on my computer for different bodies of water."

On his computer Mason has the results of every BASS tournament ever held, so he'll carefully check the results of those tournaments against the specific lake and season he's preparing for. He'll also check out what each of the top five anglers from the seasonal tournament specifically did to win, then analyze that information to see if any areas of the lake were mentioned often and what patterns were mostly used to win the top five. "I'm not looking for specific spots. Some lakes have different sections that are historically better than others. If you see many mentions of a particular arm of the lake over and over again, there must be a reason for that. Certain areas of a lake will turn on at different times than other areas, so you want to take that into consideration when you're considering places to start during practice."

During the prespawn in midspring, Mason looks outside spawning areas where the fish will be staging. "The fish will gang up as they prepare to move up to spawn. You're going to start your search in that mid-depth range of the lake. For example, in a clear-water lake, you should start fishing deeper than a stained-water lake.

"Bass are very basic—they live to spawn, eat, and survive. During the spring, they spawn. You can tailor your fishing around the stages of spawning: prespawn, spawn, and postspawn. In the fall, bass start feeding very heavily, following the shad back into the creeks, as they get stocked up for the winter. It's a very repeatable cycle that fish go through. You want to match the stage of the fish's life cycle they're in when you arrive at the lake [or river]."

Swett: On Oklahoma's Grand Lake, Swett's research on both the seasonal patterns and the weather patterns played into his success: "The week we arrived there, the temperature was 32 degrees. The next morning it was in the single digits, and it never got above 25 degrees for the rest of the week. Everybody was deepwater fishing, fishing a winter pattern. But the week before this tournament, it was in the 70-degree range. It was a very freak cold front that came through. The tournament was won on a buzzbait by Jim Morton, but I did very well on a spinnerbait. The reason why I threw a spinnerbait was because even though the surface water temperature was plummeting fast, the colder water was only a few inches deep. It's what I call an 'artificial surface temperature.' By studying the weather patterns and knowing what the average weather cycle was prior to the tournament, I knew that the water didn't have enough time to really turn over and get into a winter pattern.

Swett is always looking for common denominators. "Sometimes it's a lure. Other times it might be a location or a certain depth. You are trying to find a pattern, not necessarily specific spots. A lot of guys have the same information that you do. By digesting a lot of information and pulling out two or three common denominators, hopefully you can identify the right bait or the right section of the lake.

Local Anglers as a Resource: Buyer Beware!

It's logical to assume that anglers who live near and regularly fish tournament waters would be a great source of information for the competitive angler. Anglers who are fishing unfamiliar waters might be tempted to soak up as much local knowledge as they can get, but, like many things in life, too much of a "good thing" can kill you. Experienced bass anglers learn over time to pick and choose their sources of information carefully. They also know how to sift through the chaff to find those kernels of information that will help them round out their research on a body of water.

Scalish: "You can get very bad 'good' information from local anglers. Most local anglers are talking about [fishing] patterns that they experienced one or two times in their lifetime. They are usually not talking about patterns in the now. This is true unless it's a tournament that's taking place while you're there. Local anglers who live near a lake have a tendency to fish memories. They are sometimes unable to put together why they caught fish in a particular spot. Pattern fishing puts fish in your boat, and patterns will change and the fish will move on.

"If I tell you where to find fish and you don't catch them there, you'll have no idea how to adjust and find fish elsewhere. You didn't go through the work to find them. If you don't take the time to understand the movement of bass in a particular lake, you're done. Getting local help doesn't help you learn a lake like you need to for tournament-level success."

While Scalish doesn't rely on local angler information in general, he notes that some local tournament anglers are going to be very knowledgeable about a lake. "They know the lake inside and out. Those guys can give you incredible information. There are a lot of guys on tour who are able to get good local information, and you can win tournaments on this information. Here's the deal: Unless you know these guys personally, they are not going to give you their ace in the hole [place to fish]." He points out that local anglers might give their D+ or C fishing spots, but generally not their A+ spots.

"Local information could destroy you when you fish higher-level tournaments," adds Scalish. In his first Elite BASS tournament, he listened to a competitor who was also a friend. Scalish had what he thought was a good practice session, but his friend mentioned that he was "killing" them on a certain pattern. So, thinking he needed to get better-quality fish to win the tournament, Scalish decided to change his fishing pattern. It turned out that had he stuck to his original pattern, he more than likely would have placed better than seventh in that tournament.

Scalish points out that having a trusted small group of people to bounce fishing

Frank Scalish pulled this "quality" fish from the lily pads using a Texas-rigged YUM Lizard.
LURENET.COM

ideas off of is very important. You need a way to vent and clear your head before the tournament, but too many ideas and options can be fatal to your chances of success. "My best tournaments are the ones where I don't have preconceived notions. I let the fish dictate to me what I have to do. In a tournament on Lake Erie, I came back from eighty-ninth place to finish fourth. That's because I didn't lock myself into a pattern or certain ideas. Years ago on another Jerry Rind tournament on Kerr Reservoir, my partner and I were catching big 5-pound-plus fish on

secondary points. We thought we were going to win the tournament—we were catching 20-plus pounds of fish without even trying. Then we fished the tournament and came in with two fish. What happened? The water level on the lake came up a foot. The fish went to the back of the pockets and got into the wood. The guys that were flipping, they killed us. It was like we weren't even on the same lake! You can't lock yourself into a pattern."

Scroggins: "You meet different people from around the various regions, and it helps if you know somebody. This is a catch-22. When I first started, I always wanted to talk to them [local anglers]. Today, I don't do that nearly as much. Here's what happens: Instead of going out and finding your own fish, someone tells you where they are. Now you have to go and look at that instead of doing your own thing. If the fish are not there, then you still have to find your own fish. So, you lose a lot of your time. It's better to go out and do your own thing."

Mason: "Very seldom do local anglers win on their home body of water. A lot of times the pros will come in and find an area that locals don't fish and do very well off of it. I would say that when I go to a lake, maybe a quarter of what I fish will be based on what a local angler might tell me. These are people I know and have a relationship with. If I ask a local, it's someone I trust.

"Over time you'll meet local anglers in and around a body of water who you'll get to know and trust. Whether it's a relative, a good friend, or a co-angler you've met at another tournament, you'll establish a local network of people who can help you in your pretournament research."

Overall, Mason considers local angler resources "a double-edged sword, something you have to be really careful with. Occasionally, I will get local information. Most of the time, I don't live and die by it." If he uses local information at all, he's looking for histories of different parts of the lake or river, such as specific colors that seem to work better than others on a specific area or segment of the water.

"Some of my best friends have been co-anglers I've met over the years. At the same time, you don't want to base all you do on what locals tell you. It's very easy for locals to develop blind spots on a lake. That's why many times tournaments are won on a spot that locals don't consider to be one of the really choice fishing locations."

Howell: While very wary of local angler advice, Howell takes a "networking" approach to developing relationships. He emphasizes that over time you should try to make contact with as many people as possible in the area of the lake or river so you can begin to develop a good networking list: "Now, fifteen years later, I've got a book that's too big to even carry with me that's full of names and cards. I've got two or three people in every state who know something about anywhere I'm going to go fishing now, so I don't have to just blindly call people anymore."

Taking Notes

Keeping records on key areas to fish and noting the effects of seasonal and weather patterns on the bass is crucial to becoming a winning tournament professional. Whether you mark spots with your GPS on electronic maps, make notes on a paper map, jot observations down in a notebook, or talk into a digital tape recorder, keeping a record of your fishing experiences on a body of water is critical to success. Compiling data and

Some pros use small digital recorders like this one to record detailed notes during practice for review later. DAVID DIRKS

organizing it helps you become a highly effective competitor.

Scalish: "Any structure I find in a lake gets labeled on my GPS. Now I let my GPS harbor the information. I always carry my maps with me and mark them."

Mason: "From a preparation standpoint, there are no secrets. It's about being prepared and well-versed on what the lake is like and on the tournament conditions in the past. I'll make notes in a notebook that I carry with me, then when I get home I organize my thoughts in a more defined way. I'll take just general

notes while I'm there on the water during practice."

By the time he gets to a lake, Mason has from ten to twenty pages of handwritten notes and several maps. "I create a file folder or binder for every lake that I'm going to fish during the year. In addition to the notes, I'll have a summary page that outlines what I want to do on the lake and how to do it. How do I want to start on my first day of practice? I'll include a list of specific baits I'll need to bring with me. I have my Navionics chip and the spots marked that I think should fit the pattern for the season I'm fishing." On his Low-rance system, Mason marks the areas he noted in his pretournament study in bright blue and the fishing spots he located during practice in bright red so he can look at his screen and immediately know how each spot was found.

Swett: In addition to his written notes, Swett always carries a digital camera with him and takes pictures of specific spots that he wants to note for the current tournament as well as future ones. "If you do this, you need to keep a log of each shot, noting the specific location in relation to the lake map. This will help you to easily relate the photo to a specific area on the lake."

Howell: "I have files for each lake that are labeled for the current year. I'll add an after-tournament summary on what I should have done, what weight won the tournament, and what pattern was predominant." Over time, Howell has accumulated thick files that are rich with information that helps him to plan his fishing in any season and under any conditions. "If you fish a certain body of water long enough, you begin to learn how to fish it in all kinds of weather conditions."

The Limitations of Pretournament Research

Pretournament research, no matter how extensively done, is never foolproof.

Top professional anglers make it a point to never get too hung up on what their research is telling them. Research can help you narrow down the areas you want to check out first, depending upon seasonality, but it's never a replacement for actually just fishing.

Scalish: "I was fishing a tournament at Clear Lake in California, which I had never fished before. I researched the lake on the Internet and found out that there are some giant fish in this lake. Generally, 17 to 18 pounds of fish a day is in the money. What I didn't know until I got there was that they had sprayed the lake and had killed off most of the vegetation. Where there used to be miles and miles of vegetation that went hundreds of yards offshore, there was now little tiny, skinny strands of vegetation along the bank. What that did was make all those fish that were coming shallow to spawn more accessible. Instead of being in the thick vegetation, where they could spread out and have gobs of cover, they now were totally accessible and easy to catch, which I didn't know. I had about 18 pounds of fish a day and ended up in seventy-second place. Here I had thought I was going to get a check with no problem, but my [daily] weights weren't even close. These giant fish were roaming around, and everyone throwing swim baits was coming in contact with these huge 10-pounders."

CHAPTER TEN

Pretournament Preparation

If you've participated in or witnessed enough tournaments, you've undoubtedly seen this story unfold: A tournament angler is methodically working the water with his bait. After many successive casts, he feels the strike and pulls to set the hook. He can feel it—it's a big, heavy fish. It's a tournament-winning fish or, at the very least, a check-generating fish. The battle unfolds, with the bass doing its best to break off and the angler doing his best to bring it to the boat. Then, as suddenly as it began, the fight ends. No bass, no bait—it's gone. The angler drops to his knees, and his contorted face says it all. He knows something went wrong, and he's just put the win and the check out of reach.

What went wrong? It could have been any number of things, but most likely his line was frayed at some point near his bait. It might have had a nick in it, causing it to break off. Or maybe a nick in the top rod guide managed to chew on the line, making it weak.

Whatever it was, the angler knows he should have checked everything. But there wasn't enough time, he says to himself. Not enough time for careful pretournament inspection of his equipment? It's a tough lesson to learn.

Most of us are used to seeing the glamour and the excitement of the tournament weigh-ins. On both the local and national levels, days of practice and tournament play lead up to the "big event." What you don't see, but is absolutely necessary for a tournament angler to either win or just take home a check, is the preparation before it all begins. You don't see the hours and hours spent by pros like Terry Scroggins, making sure everything—including terminal tackle, baits, boats, and trucks—are in top running condition. It's not glamorous and it's probably not much fun, but it's the work of the successful tournament bass angler.

After your pretournament research, gathering the right terminal tackle and checking its performance, sorting and organizing the baits you deem necessary for a win, and making sure that your boat and truck are ready are critical to your success.

Preparing for a Tournament

Paul Elias spends about two full days before each tournament getting his terminal tackle

Frank Scalish gets another rod ready for practice time.
LURENET.COM

and other gear ready for fishing. "I'll take all the rods and reels out of the boat. I'll line them up and decide which ones I'm going to need for the lake. Am I going to need three flipping sticks and three cranking rods? Two spinnerbait rods and two jig rods? Once I decide on which ones I'm taking, I strip them all of line and put new line on them. Most of my time is spent going through all the tackle in my boat, trying to eliminate stuff I know I'm not going to use. I'll take two plastic containers with things I won't put in the boat but I might need during the tournament." Elias generally carries eighteen to twenty rods on the boat in any given tournament. In most general fishing situations, he has at least three spinning rods, with the balance being baitcasting rods.

For practice time, Elias generally will whittle his lure selection down as much as possible: "For instance, I may have four tackle boxes with jerkbaits. I will take all those with me to the tournament but only have one box in my boat. I try to take a good variety of those jerkbaits, then I'll decide after practice if I need to subtract from or add to my boat. I'll do that with every version of lure I have."

Terry Scroggins: "When I prepare my boat for a practice day, I like to have twenty-five or thirty rods rigged with whatever kinds of bait you could imagine. That's what practice is—to learn what they are going to bite or not bite. After three days of practice, I like to narrow it down to about ten rods. It's just a process of elimination as to what the fish are going to bite. The drop-shot, shaky-head worm is huge across the country. That's a bait that can catch you a limit and probably cash a check for you but more than likely is not going to win the event. But you have to have one of those [finesse rods] in your arsenal just for backup. I'm more of a power fisherman than anything. I like to throw crankbaits, flip heavy cover, throw a spinnerbait, and just cover a lot of water. I like to go to those types of baits, but at the same time, I'm not scared to fall back on a shaky-head or drop-shot to catch a few fish."

Sam Swett: Swett refers to the process of getting his fishing tackle ready as "getting my gear tuned to the lake." This means making sure that the line and the rods and reels match the water he will be fishing and his basic practice strategy. "When I'm doing my pretournament research, I'm making mental notes about the baits that I need to bring. When I do that, I jot them down on a list. I have about eight large containers which I start loading up with baits. Inevitably, while I'm at a tournament, there will be something that they're biting on that I don't have with me but have at home. I don't take everything, but I try to take as much as I can in anticipation of what I'll need." By the time practice comes, he's ready to start whittling down some of those baits to the ones he'll definitely need during the tournament.

Swett prefers to prepare his boat by getting to the tournament a day before

These rods are rigged and ready to go in preparation for a tournament. LURENET.COM

practice begins. "I literally pull out all the rods I have and go through my tackle. All my tackle boxes will be organized for that particular tournament." He likens the process to a mechanic who pulls out the tools he'll need to work on a specific part of a vehicle.

Swett also makes sure that he adds fresh line to all his reels. He keeps a variety of line sizes on his reels to insure he's prepared to fish whatever water conditions he finds at the tournaments. He recommends carrying 6- to 20-pound-test lines of both monofilament and fluorocarbon in 2-pound increments. "Don't let price stand in your way of buying larger spools of line. A lot of people don't respool their lines during a tournament. There are so many bad things that can happen to your line underneath the water. It's very important to keep your reels spooled with fresh line."

He recommends buying the larger spools of line, like 2,500- or 3,000-yard spools. "With smaller line spools, there is so much line waste. On smaller spools, you generally don't have enough to spool more than one reel, so buying the larger spools is more efficient and sometimes less expensive."

Swett has around thirty-six rods/reels that he brings to every tournament. "I try to keep at least a half dozen as flipping sticks and another half dozen as spinning reels for drop-shots, or shaky-head worm fishing, or any finesse-type fishing. I'll have another seven or eight spinnerbait rods that are rigged for everything from an

eighth ounce to an ounce or ounce and a quarter. You want enough rods on hand to match the conditions. Some rods are multipurpose rods. For instance, my Carolina-rigged rods are very efficient for frogging. If I'm throwing a YUM Buzz Frog, for example, I know I can throw a Carolina rig with the same rod."

"I'm always checking my drag," says Swett, "to make sure nothing sticks on my drag during practice or the tournament. On my rods, I'll take a Q-tip and run it through each guide to make sure I'm not getting any line frayed or anything that could damage the line. I'll look for splintering on the rod because I don't want to set the hook on a fish and have the rod splinter on me." Swett also carefully checks each reel to insure the ball bearings are still smooth.

Frank Scalish: "Rods are easy to maintain. I use Lemon Pledge on all my rods. The wax coating helps keep grime and gunk from sticking on your rod. Also, it slicks up the guides so they cast smoother. I'll clean the rods with a damp paper towel and then rub them down with Lemon Pledge. If a rod handle gets dirty and grimy, I use 900-grade sandpaper on it. It won't take a lot of cork off, but it will take the dirt off.

"I check the level line gear to make sure there is no grass on it. I take a Q-tip and clean the line guide. For the most part, if I have been fishing brackish water [mix of fresh and salt water], I take the reels apart and clean them." Outside of

Rigging rods is a labor of love for Sam Swett. He, like other pros, spends hours before each tournament doing it. SAM SWETT

fishing brackish water or not performing well, Scalish will break down his reels and clean and lube them once per season. "If you start hearing sounds or the reel is not performing well, then take it apart."

Scalish, like many tournament pros, spends a lot of time organizing his baits. He has containers for individual types of bait and keeps a reasonable amount of each on his boat. As he uses up baits during practices and tournaments, he'll replenish them with inventory stored in containers in his truck. When he returns

from a tournament, he'll replenish the truck inventory with the inventory kept in his basement. This way, his boat and truck inventory are always replenished and full.

"I see guys, especially nonboaters, who will waste more time looking for stuff than I could ever imagine wasting in a day. Having an unorganized system wastes enough time in the day to literally cost you a limit. I know people who throw all their soft plastics in a container. When they are fishing, they'll open the container and start hunting through it. By the end of the day,

The time to organize your baits is well before you're on the road for a tournament. DAVID DIRKS

that could cost you a half hour [of tournament time]."

A Word on Buying Tackle

There is a lot of debate over what quality of tackle you should consider acquiring for tournament fishing. The bass tackle business is a multibillion-dollar industry in the United States alone. Unlike a few decades ago, the variety of terminal tackle, baits, and lines available to bass anglers is huge and sometimes overwhelming. While you'll hardly find uniform agreement on

what types of tackle to buy, almost all tournament anglers agree on this: Buying tackle of any kind is driven by personal preference. It's what works for you that counts. It has nothing to do with how much you can spend either—it's a matter of which rod or reel feels best in your hand. This is a completely personal experience. Nonetheless, there are a few points to consider that will help you make your way through the bewildering array of modern tackle.

Swett: "The thing about fishing gear is confidence. You don't need $500 or $1,000 rod/reel combinations. They are nice and they will last the distance, and you do get what you pay for. But you'll always have the person who will pick up a $50 rod and shake it and feel it. They might like that rod. Another person can pick up the same rod and say, 'It's too flimsy' or 'It's not what I need.' A lot of it is personal preference.

"I try not to let price put a limit on me. I want to be sure I have the right equipment and the right sensitivity to do what I need to do." He emphasizes finding that combination of rod and reel that you are not only comfortable with, but also helps you stay sensitive to the fish. Your fishing equipment has to fit like a glove that is molded to your hand perfectly. For Swett, a rod is nothing more than an extension of his arm. It has to be able to allow him to feel underwater stumps, across grass or gravel, or a strike. It has to transmit what's happening under the water to him.

"Use the same reel if possible, other than changing for reel speed [ratio]. When I'm casting or retrieving, I palm the reel a lot. I want to have that same feel in my hand. I want paddles of the handle to be the same. When I lay one rod down and pick up another, I feel like I didn't make a transition [with the rod]. Although the action of the rod might change, it feels just like the last one."

Elias: "It all depends on a person's financial situation. Some people feel like they have to have the best of everything. I think with the product lines that most of these companies have today, you can find a very good rig in the middle class of the line they have. As you progress and you get better [at tournament fishing], there are features on rods and reels that you may want."

Scalish: "You are either going to have good equipment or not. Better equipment is going to translate into better feel, sensitivity, and casting capabilities. You have to pick out the best possible equipment you can afford in both rods and reels. It's going to last you longer, which makes it cheaper in the long run." Scalish points out that the critical factor of fishing better should not be underestimated: "A ten-ball-bearing reel is going to work better than a four-ball-bearing reel."

As proof of this point, Scalish has ten-ball-bearing reels that are fifteen years old that he's still using today. "Rods and reels are nothing to skimp on. I'm not saying you have to go out and buy a $350 reel, because I don't own a $350 reel. The reality is that you want to look for reels that have multiple ball bearings and good-quality construction."

Scalish prefers to fish his Powell rods at 7 feet 3 inches. He also uses the exact same brand and style of reels every time. "Every time I pick up a rod, it feels exactly the same. There's no difference. I know guys who fish with different rods and reels, but I think at that point, you're not giving yourself an advantage."

Randy Howell: Early in his career, Howell was amazed to learn how better gear helped to improve his fishing, noting "The better you fish and the better you cast, the more your confidence level goes up." If you don't have a lot of money to spend, he believes it's much better to have one very high-quality outfit than to have three cheaper ones.

Howell divides his rods into three key groups: heavy action, medium action, and spinning rods. The stiff heavy-action rods are for power, for setting the hook on set-ups like Carolina rigs, jigs, flipping, and pitching. Medium-action 6 1/2- to 7-foot rods are used for spinnerbaits, jerkbaits, and topwater baits. He feels that medium- or medium/heavy-action rods in those sizes are good all-around rods to have. Howell rounds out his choices by emphasizing that you need to have spinning rods. He prefers 6-foot-10-inch or 7-foot medium- to medium/heavy-action spinning rods.

More about Fishing Lines

Taking care of line is critical. Store your line in an area that will not subject it to extreme heat. Heat deteriorates the quality and strength of a line. It doesn't take much to nick line, and you're probably not going to see the nick until it's way too late. Is it worth losing a fish that could help you win a tournament? Ask anyone who has lost a fish because of a nick in the line, and you might see tears well up in their eyes.

Swett: "I keep my fishing line in an ice cooler. That way, if there is a major change in conditions, it's not going to affect the line." In either extreme heat or cold, an insulated cooler will help moderate the air temperature affecting the line. "Your fishing line is your life line—it's what puts fish in the boat. So you want to take care of your fishing line." After a tournament, don't leave your fishing line on the boat or in the basement. Bring it in to where you can keep it in a 65- to 85-degree air temperature area.

Making sure you have a variety of line sizes is critical, according to Swett. "I use different lines for different applications. I make sure I pack the amount and variety of line I need. If I'm going to predominately do finesse fishing, I bring enough small-diameter line. If I'm going to be frog fishing or fishing super-heavy cover, I bring plenty of braided line. If I'm throwing topwater, then I also bring plenty of monofilament line. For bottom fishing, like with a Carolina rig or tube fishing, I'll have plenty of fluorocarbon."

For topwater fishing, monofilament is the way to go, primarily because it floats. When fishing topwater lures like a Pop'R or Zara Spook, Swett sometimes uses a thicker-diameter monofilament line. "Some people will tell me, 'I can't get the topwater action of my bait to work properly.' That's because they are sometimes using 20-pound fluorocarbon line [that sinks]."

Scalish: "I use braided lines for Carolina-rigging, throwing Super Spooks, and for throwing rattle baits. For Carolina-rigging, braided line is my main line with a monofilament leader." Scalish uses a monofilament line leader for this setup primarily because monofilament, as opposed to

Applying a line conditioner before a tournament keeps your line and reel in good working order. DAVID DIRKS

fluorocarbon leader, floats and keeps his rig off the bottom better. Given that braided lines have little or no stretch, Scalish prefers the extra sensitivity you get by using braid for a Carolina rig.

"For my flipping, drop-shot, and Texas-rigged worms, or any soft plastic presentation, I'm using fluorocarbon exclusively. Fluorocarbon offers less stretch, better sensitivity, and better hookups [than using monofilament]. For crankbaits, spinnerbaits, and jerkbaits, I use Silver Thread, which is a monofilament. The only time I'll change to fluorocarbon with my crankbaits and jerkbaits is if I want to get them down deeper. The characteristics of fluorocarbon will help me gain a little more depth. Monofilament will also keep your suspending jerkbaits suspended."

Howell: "I was a light-line man in my early years [on the tour] for sight fishing. As I got into areas that were rougher and tougher with brush, trees, and a lot of cover, I started using bigger, heavier tackle. As I did that, I started realizing that the fish never seemed to be too sensitive about my [heavier] line. It was more about how I presented the bait, how I read the fish, and how I moved [the bait] and did things at the right times. When you're fishing against the clock, if you can cut down on the time it takes to catch one, the faster you can go after another one."

Howell will generally use a 30-pound Spiderwire Stealth braid for his startup presentations. He'll match the line with a 7-foot medium/heavy-action baitcasting rod with a fast-retrieve reel, because when every second counts, you want to be able to pull the bait back to the boat and then get it back out there as fast as you can.

Checking Your Bass Boat

Not unlike race car drivers who depend totally on the operating performance of their vehicles, tournament anglers need their boats to be in top shape prior to a tournament. Having a mechanical breakdown during a tournament means the loss of precious time that could have been spent catching a quality limit of fish. Fortunately, most problems are clearly preventable or can be taken care of well before the tournament starts.

Swett: Swett does all his boat checking and maintenance at least a week before a tournament and the day before he leaves for practice, just to make sure everything is in top performance shape. This kind of maintenance discipline gives him plenty of time to fix any problems that come up well before the tournament starts.

"Inspect the batteries, checking for any corrosion. Make sure that they are fully charged each day of both practice and tournament time. Turn on your aerators and bilge pump to make sure they are working properly. Also check the electrical connection on both the aerator and the bilge pump, making sure there is no corrosion buildup. Check all the circuit breaker terminals for corrosion.

Checking battery connections is something no pro skips. Like most pros, Terry Scroggins checks his every day. DAVID DIRKS

Scroggins carefully checks his engine and the mounts that hold it in place as part of his pretournament preparation. DAVID DIRKS

"Check all the running lights. Make sure the engine fires up on the first try, and check that the kill switch is working well too. Run all the GPS and other electronics."

As for the appearance of your boat, Swett says, "If you're going to try to obtain sponsors or already have sponsors, it is crucial to have a clean boat and equipment." Nothing says professionalism louder than equipment that is always clean and presentable in public.

Scroggins: "In cold weather, like anything less than 40 degrees, you really need to let your engine warm up before you use it for a good five to ten minutes. I actually blew an engine up one time. It was 18 degrees and I didn't let it warm up as long as I should have. I made it about a mile down the river and blew the engine."

Scalish: Scalish recommends checking the motor and jackplate bolts and making sure they are tight. He always checks everything that holds the motor to the boat and the jackplate. "These boats take a beating, and the bolts will loosen up on the jackplate or loosen up on the transom."

Organizing Your Bass Boat

Almost all pros have their own personal way of organizing their boat and the tackle

Having your rods and favorite baits ready for action is critical. Note how this rod is labeled with a 12 to indicate what pound test line is on the reel. SAM SWETT

BOAT ITEMS CHECKLIST

Have a special "boat kit" on board that contains tools and other items to help you keep your boat in top running condition or make a quick repair while on the water. Here's a list of some of the items typically in this kit.

- Superglue
- Electrical tape
- Spare washers
- Bolts
- Nuts
- Crescent wrench
- Pair of wire cutters
- Channel lock
- Prop wrenches

- Phillips and flat-head screwdrivers
- Duct tape
- Pair of very sharp scissors
- Pliers
- Set of ruby sharpening stones
- Zap-A-Gap (for securing knots)
- Allen keys
- Socket wrench set
- Electrician's tape

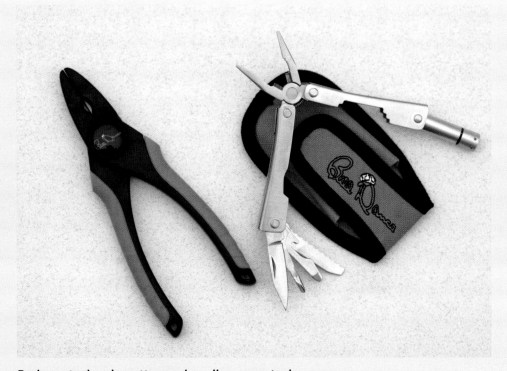

Basic pro tools: wire cutters and an all-purpose tool. DAVID DIRKS

- Cordless drill (to tighten screws without having to do it by hand and eat into your practice or tournament time)

- Black, brown, olive, and red Sharpie markers (for modifying color shades on baits)

- Sunscreen, extra sunglasses, and rain jacket

- (Don't depend on your fishing partner to bring his or her own Life jacket. Always have an extra one.)

- Buy good-quality tools that can hold up to the abuse of moisture, and keep them in a watertight box.

that goes with it for tournament fishing. But for all their differences, they all agree that an organized boat allows you to fish more efficiently and effectively. Efficiency is about doing things right, and effectiveness is about doing the right things. You'll develop your own organizing style, but your goal will be the same as your nearby competitor: keeping your gear organized so that you can quickly switch tackle, baits, and techniques quickly. This enables you to spend more time fishing than wasting valuable tournament time trying to locate what you need.

Scalish: "I'm tackle heavy in my boat. I carry a lot of stuff for about every scenario you could imagine. But, it's all labeled and it's all in small plastic boxes. It's too much trouble for me to go to a tournament, unload my boat, and put in just what I need for that tournament, then have to pack up and go to my next tournament and reload the boat. I don't do that."

Scalish says that as long as your tackle

and baits are well-organized on the boat and you can get to them easily, there's no reason not to load your boat up with as much as it can safely hold.

Scroggins: "You want to be careful how you load your boat. You want to have all your heavy stuff toward the back of the boat, like your plastic worms and hardbaits. I like to have everything I'm going to use in the front of the boat so I don't have to take more than a step to get to it. At the same time, you don't want a lot of heavy weight in the front of the boat. What that does is make the front of the boat heavy to where you can't make it lift. You need to get the nose of the boat out of the water to run fast. If you're on a long run and you have a lot of weight in the boat, you can actually lose 4 to 5 miles per hour, which is critical in a tournament.

"I might also have twenty-five tackle boxes with me in the truck and boat. When it comes down to the tournament, I like to just get down to no more than seven or eight boxes in the boat. Have those labeled so you can grab what you need."

Scroggins likes to have all his crankbait rods packed on one side of the boat and his worm- and jig-fishing rods on the other.

For Swett, the organization of his boat is based on his plan for how he will approach his practice time. Most often, he'll bring more gear and baits during practice and use that time to determine what gear he won't need to bring during the tournament. As the practice progresses, Swett repacks his boat each day, adding or removing tackle and baits as necessary: "I let the practice day tell me what gear I'll need for the next day and reload my boat accordingly."

Swett suggests developing a routine for packing your tackle into both your boat and towing vehicle. The more you get into a routine for organizing and packing, the more sensitive you'll be to whether you're missing something before you hit the road. "You have to find what works for you."

Mental Preparation

Most competitive anglers understand that some anxiety just before a tournament is

Keeping your boat organized during practice time makes for less work when tournament time comes around. DAVID DIRKS

a natural occurrence. Sometimes it's more or less about how much confidence you have in your abilities to fish a particular lake. High confidence levels can reduce anxiety and help you mentally prepare for the tournament. Reduced anxiety means that you'll fish more effectively and be able to make clearer decisions. As we will see in future chapters, it's decision-making that separates the winners from the losers.

Swett: "After seventeen years of tournament fishing, I still get butterflies in my stomach at takeoff time in the morning [of a tournament]. It's a make or break time, and the tournament is getting ready to start. One thing I learned, and I learned it from my dad, is that I've got to have fun. The more fun I have fishing, the more my natural ability comes back out. Then I can rely on myself to catch fish and not be intimidated by everyone else."

Scalish does two things when he finds himself anxious either before or during a tournament: 1) He finds a good comedy movie and watches it. He says it helps him forget about the anxiety before a tournament—he just laughs it off. 2) If he's having a tough time, he'll work to bring his positive mental attitude back by remembering all the tournaments he's won and the high points of his career. In competitive angling, having high levels of anxiety or self-doubt will not help you win a tournament or even place in a money spot.

"It's easy to [mentally] unravel," says Scalish. "And the bigger the [tournament] stakes, the easier it is to unravel. You can't do that because it'll affect your judgment on the water."

CHAPTER ELEVEN

Pretournament Practice

Practice time for a tournament bass angler is one of the most critical points in the buildup to the "big day." Well before the cameras begin rolling or the fans start to show up, the professional angler is putting his boat in the water. It's a time for figuring out the fish: What are they doing now? Where are they? What will it take to get them to bite? Where are the "limit" fish? Where are the "quality" fish? Do I have the right tackle prepared? What am I missing? What part of the lake or river is "hot"? How many quality spots can I find before the tournament begins? Where do I start?

These questions, and the many more that follow, will lead to a tournament victory if answered correctly. During practice time, all of your competitors will try to answer the same questions. So while all competitors may start on a level playing field, once practice time begins, the field begins to get uneven. Those who know how to use their practice time effectively will find themselves fishing and winning more consistently.

Effective Practice Time

Terry Scroggins: "What I'll do in practice is find four or five areas in three days where I think I can catch them [fish] pretty good. I'll start on those spots and try to catch five good ones. And then I'll expand on that and keep practicing throughout the tournament, trying to find new locations where I can catch another limit the next day." To Scroggins, it's the never-ending practice time. And it's a winning strategy that helps keep him in the top of most of the tournaments he fishes. "You have to be open-minded and not afraid to fish new water during the tournament. In other words, when the tournament starts, my practice is not over—I keep practicing."

For fishing a body of water you're not so familiar with, Scroggins recommends limiting yourself to a 10-mile area and learning that area very well before you go to other parts of the lake. "A big body of water can overwhelm you. You go there and say, 'Wow, how am I going to cover this?' Before you know it, you're trying to cover all of it. It'll end up messing you up instead of helping you."

Scroggins divides a lake into three sections and fishes the farthest section from the boat ramp on practice day one. On the second day of practice, he'll hit the middle third of that distance, and on the last day of practice, he fishes the area closest to the launch ramp. This not only gives him a chance to cover a lot of water, but it also has a practical side: getting him to the tournament briefing on time. Most tournaments conduct mandatory briefings on the last day of practice.

As for specific places to concentrate on, Scroggins offers this advice: "If I go to a lake that I don't know anything about, the number one thing I'll do is fish all the boat ramps and all the marinas. That's where all the fish get turned loose [after tournaments]. Keep in mind that they have club tournaments and local boat tournaments [during the year]. A big population of fish gets turned loose in those places." It's a good place to start when you haven't fished a body of water that much.

"What I do in practice is try to find two or three spots a day. Over three days of practice, you've got at least six spots. If you have six spots going into a tournament, that's a very productive practice. On the first day of the tournament, I'll fish those six spots and catch what I can catch. As I'm moving around, I'm still looking for new water." Scroggins uses his tournament time as additional "practice" time as well. He's always on the lookout for more good-producing spots to fish. It helps him set up his plan of attack for each tournament day. Scroggins doesn't worry about what he'll do at the beginning of each day, since he's already done his homework the day before.

He also pays a lot of attention to the contours and geographic layout of the lake: "If it has high banks and a lot of hills around it, you can normally fish tighter to the bank. If it's a low-lying lake, a flatter lake, then I like to fish more offshore."

To gain more confidence during your practice time, Scroggins recommends starting off with light-line tackle, like a shaky-head drop-shot, and catching numbers of fish. "Even though it's a small fish bait, I've caught a lot of 7- to 8-pound fish on a shaky-head worm. That will generate more bites and give you more confidence in an area. Then you can come back with a crankbait or spinnerbait and try to catch a bigger fish. You've got to know they live there before you can catch them."

As for the use of electronics during practice, Scroggins says, "You've got to trust your electronics 100 percent. If it says there are fish down there, you've got to believe it and make them bite. If you start doubting your equipment, you're in trouble."

Scroggins believes it's critical, despite your experience and history with a particular body of water, to fish in the

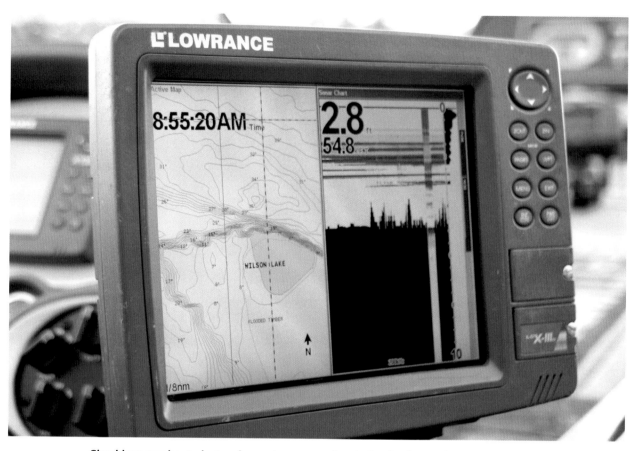

Checking your boat electronics system every day during both practice and tournament time will help you build confidence in it. DAVID DIRKS

present and not in the past. "You can also get in trouble by knowing too much. It doesn't matter if you're fishing at home or 2,000 miles away from home—you have to fish in the moment. You have to fish to what's going on in the present time.

"In practice you might have found fish tight to cover or on a ledge—the sun is up high, and there are slick water conditions with a little bit of current moving. On the first day of the tournament, it's now cloudy, windy, with no current moving. They are not going to be where you found them during practice. They might be 100

yards away doing something different." This is another example of why it's critical to keep an open mind and be prepared for changing conditions.

Jimmy Mason: "A lot depends on how much practice time you have and how much experience you have on any given body of water. In the Elite Series, we have basically two and a half days of practice. A lot of the lakes, especially in the first couple of years [on the tour], most anglers have never been to. In those situations, the best thing to do is pick one section of the lake—be it one creek or one 10-mile section [of lake]—and spend the first two days really learning it. If the first day [of practice] goes well, then I will spend the second day in the same general area trying to refine the pattern more. I'm trying to find more areas close by that match the pattern." Mason ties that in with the local long-range weather forecast for the tournament. Things like cold fronts and drops or rises in water levels can play a major role as to what the fish will do.

On a lake Mason has never fished, he spends the first day just learning the lake—riding around it, never making a cast. "I'll look at all the areas that caught my eye during the pretournament preparation. What's the water color? Is there more or less cover than I thought it was going to be?" He's also looking for bait, paying close attention to his electronics to see if the bait is at a higher or lower depth in the water. Mason is disciplined and takes handwritten notes during each practice day. He sometimes even uses a digital recorder to document what he's learning about the lake.

If he decides to fish another section of the lake based on the results from his first practice day, he'll compare the two practice days. Which practice area provided the better results? On his third day of practice, he'll focus his attention on the area that shows the greatest promise of fishing results.

How do you prioritize which spots you start with on day one of the tournament? "Everyone at the Elite Series is a heck of a fisherman," Mason says. "Everybody is very good mechanically. What separates who wins and who finishes badly is strictly based on decision-making. Every spot you go to is a calculated risk."

Randy Howell: Based on his research, Howell will generally pick a few areas that match the type of seasonal fishing expected for that lake. If the fish are shallow, for example, he'll look for the most promising shallow areas. Once he arrives on the lake for practice, his priority is getting to those areas and exploring them. "I'm looking at my Lowrance electronics, figuring out the contour of the area. Then I'll start fishing. If I start catching some, I then start figuring out if there is a pattern here. The first day [of practice] is all about the areas I researched." Howell's initial plan either helps him find productive water or helps him eliminate water.

On his second day of practice, he is applying what he has learned from day one to start his day of fishing. "I'm more of a natural instinct, intuitive fisherman. I learn more by riding around [the water] and looking. That's not something you learn by reading books or watching videos. You get that only by spending time on the water."

As Howell travels the country doing fishing seminars, he often hears that one of the biggest mistakes many weekend, local, and regional tournament anglers make is overfishing an area. Overfishing just leads to inconsistent results. You might catch multiple fish in one area one day, but then come back the following day and catch

You'll find hundreds of books available on basic bass fishing today. Tour pros recommend a constant learning program. DAVID DIRKS

next to nothing. "When I practice and go into an area and start fishing, if I'm fishing a bait that's a reaction bait like a crankbait or Rat-L-Trap, I'll keep my hooks on the bait to start with." After he catches a fish or two in an area, Howell knows enough to stop fishing that area and start fishing another. He also knows that if he was able to catch a few fish there, there are probably more in the area. It generally doesn't pay to disturb all the fish by catching them during practice time.

To reduce catches during practices, Howell will clip the barbs off his lure,

leaving just enough bend in the hook to allow him to feel a fish but not catch it. This is a common tactic in tournament circles.

To find out what the fish are keying on for food, Howell will examine a fish's mouth to see if there is any baitfish or crawfish in it. Sometimes, it's paying attention to those little things that can help you determine what the fish want. "Seeing is believing," says Howell.

Paul Elias: "I usually pick an area of the lake that's been producing [fish]." For example, Elias might find out that most of

Paul Elias displays two excellent examples of tournament "quality" fish. LURENET.COM

the fish are being taken from up the river channel and that there are several creeks connected to the river. He will then go and concentrate on as many creeks as possible during one practice day. If he finds those areas producing well, he might decide to spend most of his practice time exploring the river and its feeder creeks. He will also try to find something close to the weigh-in area.

"I feel if I find one good area a day in practice, I'm doing well. That gives me three areas in the tournament. If it's a hard tournament and you've only found one place to get good bites in, you go there and stay. You try to get as good a stringer as you can pick out. There are times after the practice period that you realize that you didn't really accomplish a strategy to win the tournament. You need to survive this tournament, try to get a check, and go on to the next one."

Elias has never been one to try to cover the whole lake. "I've always picked an area of a lake that I thought I would like to fish. I would really work on that area. I very seldom run a real long way [from the boat launch]. I try to put something together within a reasonable distance from the takeoff."

If he knows it's going to take a lot of fish to win a particular tournament, he feels he needs to have at least ten to fifteen bites a day in practice in order to feel that he's going to do well. "If I go to a lake that I know that 10 to 12 pounds a day is solid [for a win] and there is an abundance of

fish, that's a practice time that really needs to be watched closely. What happens on those types of lakes is that [anglers] are sticking a lot of fish in the practice period because they are trying to find the better-sized fish. I found that if most of the fish are averaging 1.5 pounds and every now and then you catch a 4-pounder, if you've caught that 4-pounder, you've really hurt yourself.

"You've got to be both lucky and good. You're not going to eliminate the luck factor on those 4- to 6-pounders when everyone else is catching 2-pounders. But, there is a difference between luck and setting a pattern that's giving you 15 pounds [of fish] a day in a 10- to 12-pound-average tournament. That's not luck, that's skill."

Two things Elias always studies during practice time are the baitfish and water temperature. "I'm always looking for the baitfish. They [the bass] are going to be near the baitfish. Now, it may not be schools of shad. It may be an obvious thing that bluegills are hanging around. Sometimes you'll see a lot of bluegills around the bank or hanging around a dock. Bass eat bluegills, so there'll be some bass around.

"The other major thing is water temperature, especially in the spring and fall. If you can find an area on the lake in the early spring or late fall that might be a little warmer and there is a good mixture of baitfish in there, you're probably going to catch some fish."

Elias also pays close attention to his electronics during practice. "A bass fisherman is always looking at his electronics. I don't care if he's in 2 feet of water. There's always that time when all of a sudden you see something on your depth finder. It might have gone from 2 feet [in depth] to 3.5 feet. A little break like that in shallow water can be just like a creek ledge in 12 to 20 feet of water. So those are the kinds of things you need to be constantly monitoring for and deciding whether it's worth looking at. The depth finders are so sophisticated now that they can draw a stump out [on the monitor]. If you're fishing a lake that doesn't have a lot of cover and you're watching your depth finder in 5 feet of water and it draws a stump out, that's something I'm going to want to check out. I'm going to circle around and fish that stump." It only takes a few seconds to miss some structure or cover that you just drove over.

When fishing a lake that receives heavy pressure from the great number of tournaments hosted on it, Elias will try a different tactic. "If there has been tournament after tournament and there's really no place [for fish] to hide, you need to find something different. Sometimes I'm fortunate in that respect because 90 percent of the guys are beating the banks or beating the shallow water. So if there is a deeper bite, that'll help me. For the most part, when a lake is beat up like that, you've got to go to spinning gear using a shaky-head worm or drop-shot and just finesse out a limit.

"The main thing is not to lose your confidence and don't get negative. Stay as positive as you can no matter how many things are going wrong or how tough the fishing is. It's possible to catch up."

In the end, it all comes down to experience and instinct. "There's an instinct that I can't explain that I get. I'll go into a creek or a cove and it just looks right to me. And it usually works out that it is."

Sam Swett: "If it's a lake I've never been to and I have unlimited practice time, I'll cruise the lake. I want to determine visually what the lake has to offer. If the midsection of a lake is reported to have stained water, I want to see what they are calling 'stained water.' Sometimes it could be clear water. 'Clear water' in south Louisiana means you can see 2 or 3 feet. 'Clear water' up in New York means you can see 10 to 20 feet deep."

Swett also wants to identify the types of vegetation the water has and check out the bottom. Is it clay? Gravel? Chunk rock? He will write this type of information about a body of water on his maps. This is critical, especially if the information you find during practice isn't printed on your maps. "If the map just notes that there are ledges in a spot but I'm graphing stumps and grass on it, I'm going to write that information on the map." These kinds of detail-oriented notes on lake or river characteristics provide you with a valuable database of information that will continue to grow as you learn that body of water over time. Top-performing pros never underestimate this kind of discipline, especially early in their careers.

Swett takes notes all during practice. "Some of my maps look horrible because I make marks about anything that relates to a particular spot. If I found a brush pile, I'll want to mark that on my map and make a few notes that will give me coordinates on that spot. I don't want to rely just on my GPS. I want both my GPS and my handwritten notes to get me back to that exact spot."

Swett recalls a tournament practice he had a few years ago when he found a clear-water bayou and was throwing a spinnerbait. "I found that I could catch fish in every irregular feature in the grass line. A lot of the irregular features were caused by either a stump or a branch extending out from the shoreline that was catching the grass and making these small eddies. But you couldn't see them until you were right on top of them with the boat. I caught two or three quality fish. I just took my time and jotted down [on the map] every place I found these irregular features." That kind of detail allowed Swett to know exactly where to find each of these features and when to throw to them. It's what helped him win that tournament.

If time is limited, Swett will make an educated guess as to what section of the lake he needs to be on. "Sometimes anglers want to search one end of the lake to another and try to know everything there is about that water. Sometimes there's just not enough time." For example, pulling into a creek channel and spending your practice time getting a deeper understanding about all aspects of that creek, as opposed to blasting your way around the lake in search of water, is one strategy for managing your practice time effectively.

Slow down and carefully troll through the area, using your electronics to take note of every detail that could help you determine where the fish might be holding. If you have a very short period of time to practice, learn one section of the lake very well and find out during practice what's working in that section. In normal two- or three-day practices, Swett tries to eliminate as much water as possible so he can move into the tournament with a few select spots. The outcome from practice should be a high degree of fishing confidence in a smaller number of spots on a body of water.

During practice, Swett limits the amount of fish he will catch in a spot. His point is that he doesn't want to catch all the fish and "sore mouth" them to his baits. "Sometimes I don't even want to show the fish my bait. If they hit it and they feel that hard plastic from a jerkbait, crankbait, or something else, they might not hit it again. So if I go into a spot and catch two or three quality fish, I'll stop fishing. Then I'll start idling the boat around the area with the trolling motor to learn as much about the area as possible."

Swett believes you need to work as hard as you can during practice and feel confident about what you found. "Until you get that confidence level, keep practicing."

He points out, however, that you can have a great practice and still end up not winning anything if you're in "information overload" with too much practice. Like anything else in bass tournament fishing, knowing when enough practice is enough is key to making a winning finish. "Some anglers can start second-guessing themselves as to where they should go [when the tournament starts]. That goes back to the problem of expanding too much territory during practice."

Being on a lake that is 70 miles long, where you might find fish in spots that are very distant from each other, is part of the challenge. Given the limited time you have to fish, being able to clearly decide which spots you want to focus on during the tournament is critical for winning placement. Otherwise, as Swett points out, you'll spend more time trying to decide where to fish instead of fishing.

"Really try to focus on the matter at hand. If you've had a successful practice, really define what you found." That means looking for areas that you could use for backups that are near your key fishing spots. On large bodies of water, it's a matter of determining how much fishing time you are losing by moving from spot

You can't be intimidated by the prospect of fishing a huge lake, like Lake Erie pictured here. LURENET.COM

to spot. Concentrate your efforts on just a few key areas so that you don't lose valuable fishing time. There's nothing worse than spending more time traveling than actually fishing.

Swett takes a page from pro Rick Clunn: "Rick taught me the adage 'If you think about it, do it.' Rick believes that somewhere in your past you were in a similar situation where something worked for you. Your mind recalls that somehow. You never want to be in the 'would of, could of, should of' situation. Some would plainly call that more of a 'gut feel' for approaching a certain fishing situation. Whatever you call it, it's the application of your total fishing experience that will help you win tournaments."

At the end of every practice day, Swett takes a good long walk. It helps him accomplish two important things: relieve stress and clear his head. This ultimately allows him to mentally play back the practice day with a clear focus on what happened. With a clear and stress-free mind, he's able to remember things that he might have otherwise overlooked about practice.

While pretournament research and planning is key to success, keeping an open mind is even more important, says Swett. "Always keep your mind open. Don't go into a tournament based on your pretournament information only. Make sure you let the fish, the conditions, and the environment dictate how you need to make adjustments."

Frank Scalish: Scalish believes that the best way to deal with the first practice day is to hit it hard. "You've got to get up early and be on the water when the sun is coming up. You've got to be ready to make it count. On the first practice day, you've got to spend every minute you can on the water. Sometimes, your research and hunches pay off and you immediately find the right pattern. Then you can spend the rest of your practice time honing in on your better-quality bites and/or finding more spots."

He reminds us that despite our best research and preparation, there's no substitute for fishing "in the now." "This is what the water looks like *now*. Maybe *now* is different from the last time I was here. Or maybe the water level is up or down since I did my research. Sometimes the best thing to do is not make that first cast after you launch your boat. Sometimes it's OK to sit there and drive around and look the water over."

A tournament on Smith Lake in Alabama illustrates Scalish's point: "I had never been there in my life. I started to catch a few fish in practice but nothing to write home about. What I was doing in practice was deep-jigging for spotted bass, focusing on channel bends and bluff walls. As the practice days went on, that bite was dying on me. I couldn't figure out how to be consistent. Every now and then I'd catch a good fish. On tournament day I ran to a channel bend, a bluff bend, and I start fishing and didn't get bit. I had gotten a few bites there during practice but no bites during the tournament. So I decided to work the channel out to a gravel point. I caught a 4-pounder on that gravel point. So then I decided to run secondary points, and I blasted them. I had one of the biggest stringers of the whole tournament. I had never fished any of that water in practice. It was a completely different bite, and it was the mother lode of bites.

"I got so focused on [fishing] the bluffs and channel bends that I was driving by the secondary points to get to the next channel bend or bluff. Bass break the rules, and you've got to figure them out. A failure in practice is not a failure in the tournament—it's just a way of narrowing down water."

If during practice Scalish finds a pattern that is working—for example, cranking or flipping—he'll try something else. His point is clear: Don't get stuck on just one pattern during practice that happens to be working well. Practice is time to find out what other patterns may also work.

"If I already know how to catch them, then I need to figure out how to get better-quality fish. That's tournament fishing. Tournament fishing is not a numbers game. You only need five bites, but you need the best five bites. When I won the BASS Buffalo tournament, I went out and practiced and was catching about seventy bass a day. They were all between 1.75 pounds and 2.75 pounds. After the first practice day, I went back to my room and

thought: This isn't going to win it. I need a 4-pound average [per fish] to win it. So I told myself to bail on what I was doing in practice and check something else. Sure enough, I went 20 feet deeper than I was during practice and I caught a 5-pound fish." The rest is history, as Scalish continued to find quality fish that enabled him to win the tournament.

"If I'm deep-structure fishing, usually a summer pattern or a winter pattern, and I catch one [fish], dollars-to-a-donut it's loaded with fish." Winter deepwater patterns provide access to even greater numbers of fish. "If I'm fishing shallow and flipping, I won't set up on a fish. I'll let him take the bait and pull up on it a few times to see how heavy the fish is. But I won't hook them." During practice, Scalish likes to hook only about every fifth fish or so, in order to get a good look at the quality of the fish in that spot.

"The more time you spend fishing and the more experience you have on the water, the better you can relate to conditions you'll encounter during any tournament. The minute you begin to get smarter than the fish, that's when you have problems. That's when you start second-guessing yourself instead of following what your brain and experience are telling you."

Common Practice Mistakes

There are some things that tournament anglers may do that can put a damper on their overall performance. Here are a few of the more common practice mistakes that touring bass pros witness all the time while on the water:

Over-catching fish. There's always the guy who says, "I caught fifteen fish in this spot during practice." Sure, he probably caught every one of them, but this is not a standard practice among professional bass anglers. Just catch a few and then spend the time learning the features of that particular area of water.

Going to areas that you did well in many tournaments ago. Old habits die hard, and letting go of spots that might have produced well in the past is a difficult thing to do. It's natural to have confidence in an area that has produced well for you before. Top bass pros know when to let that area go when they can't find the pattern to make it produce.

Lack of patience. Should I go or should I stay? How many times have you left an area only to hear that some anglers came after you and loaded up their boat with good fish? Or vice versa—when you stayed and the fish never turned on? "It's one of the hardest mind games that fishermen have to overcome." Most professional anglers recommend following your experience, and therefore your gut instinct, on when to stay or leave a particular spot.

To those who say, "We flipped all day and didn't catch much of anything," Scalish responds with, "Then why were you flipping all day?" He advises that if the

technique you're using isn't working after an hour or so, change it to something else. "People can get caught in a rut during practice. Practice is exactly that—practice."

Not using your electronic locator because you are fishing shallow or fishing blowdowns in shallow water. Explains Scalish, "They'll fish thirty blowdowns and catch fish on three of them. Turns out that if they had their locator on, they would have found out that there was a little ditch that ran into those three blowdowns. Had they known that, they could have idled [their boat] down that blowdown bank and put a GPS coordinate on only those blowdowns that had ditches running to them. Then when tournament time comes, they are going to fish the productive blowdowns instead of the unproductive blowdowns."

Overlooking some of the smaller, more subtle changes in structure. The only way to find those structural breaks is by using your electronics. According to Scalish, most anglers are looking for the big structural breaks, like a sharp change in depth from, say, 10 to 20 feet. "That's a good structural break, however—a structural break is any change in contour. It doesn't matter if it's 2 feet or 1 foot."

Changing lures or lure colors too often or too soon. Scalish tells the story of the angler who catches a bass on a crankbait, and it's hooked on the last treble hook: "He's got one tiny hook in his mouth; he doesn't even have the whole treble hook in his mouth. A lot of people will assume a color change will get a more aggressive bite. In some instances, that is true. The reality is, [the fish] saw that color and struck at that color. He just struck at it poorly." In this situation, Scalish will consider changing from a bait that rattles to a bait that doesn't.

Underestimating the effects of weather. "Weather can keep you from fishing," says Scalish. "Weather has kept me off of Lake Erie [for practice] because of waves and wind. It's kept me off of Santee-Cooper because of lightning storms and tornados. That can very easily happen—don't think it doesn't. The next day you can get on the water, you have to keep that storm in mind. It's going to change the water clarity in certain parts of the lake. If I want to fish the east side of the lake and the storm blew in from the west, chances are the east side of the lake is going to be muddy. That's because of the wind. The lakes down south are very susceptible to muddy water conditions. In muddy water, [the fish] don't bite very well." However, Scalish notes that lakes outside of the South that have dirty or muddy water conditions will often offer the tournament angler a great fish bite.

What to Do When Practice Doesn't Go Well

Tournament practice time can provide a different outcome for different anglers. Practice time is invaluable to the tournament pro but is also susceptible to the same variables as the tournament time itself. Changes in weather, seasonal influences, rising water or low water, and other variables can make practice seem a breeze or a nightmare. Practice is all about finding both "quality" fish (lunkers 4 pounds or better) and "limit" fish (smaller fish but many of them). With as much that can go wrong as can go right during a practice, it's the angler who can recover from a less-than-perfect practice who wins tournaments and cashes checks.

Elias: Elias doesn't confide in too many anglers when on the tour. However, there is a handful who he knows well and can discuss things with in trust and confidence. He'll take the time to compare notes with those confidants and use that information to determine his game plan for the tournament.

"When I'm not catching them [during practice], I always try to keep an open mind." He recalls a tournament where he was in the top ten after day one but fell down some after day two and was struggling on day three. "I just decided that if I'm going down, I'm going down swinging, doing what I'm best at and enjoy doing. So I went out and started throwing a crankbait, and I caught a 20-pound stringer and won the tournament. Normally, when I'm struggling during a tournament, I'll rely on my [fishing] strengths and bear down with that.

"If I've spent two and a half days practicing and I've done no good, I'm not going to go out there, do the same thing, and expect a different result. I'm going to change up, make a decision, put my trolling motor down, and go fishing. I'm not going to run and gun. A high percentage of the time it'll work out if you put your trolling motor down and fish."

Mason: "If a practice doesn't go well, then you have to make a decision: Do I pick another section of the lake? Or do I try to find the fish in the section I originally picked? I'm about fifty-fifty on that." Mason will remain in an area if he feels that its history shows that it is a strong fish producer. What he changes is his approach to fishing that area.

"There are different ways to approach [a bad practice]. You have one of two options: You either start the next day as a practice day, or go to the areas on the lake that fit your most confident style of fishing. Most of the time, I'll look for areas where I can fish a shallow crankbait and cover a lot of water quickly. What that does is allow you to fish isolated, shallow targets in a manner that you're covering a lot of water." Mason doesn't hesitate to put a shaky-head worm on and finesse fish if practice hasn't gone well. "Generally, when you do those techniques all day, you'll catch enough [fish] to survive."

Mason believes that one of the most important things you can do in a bad practice situation is to stay calm. "Settle down and fish. You're not going to catch any fish running around all day. If you are struggling and you don't have anything going, the worst thing you could do is run and fish one spot for five minutes and then fish another one for five minutes.

"A good example of that is the first major tournament I ever won. It was the American Bass Anglers National Championship back in 2003. I did not have the greatest practice, and the bad thing was it was on my home lake. It was on Wheeler Lake with about 500 people in the tournament. It was a really big event. First place was $60,000, so at the time, it was the biggest tournament I had ever fished. After the practice, my only goal was to get a check. I wanted to finish in the top 50. That night at the registration meeting, I drew boat number one. Driving home, I knew that I had first shot at any spot I wanted on that lake, so I basically picked the areas I had the most confidence in and went to first. Within two or three casts, I caught a nice fish and started the morning off well. I caught three nice fish in the morning. So within the first hour, I went from having a fairly tough practice to having three nice fish in the live well. That kind of cued me in to what other places I knew were just like that. By the end of the day, I put together a nice bag [of fish]."

Mason was the leader for all three days and won the tournament by 9 pounds. "That was the win that started my career."

Jimmy Mason applies what he learned during pretournament practice to gain a significant competitive edge. LURENET.COM

Howell: "You have to fish every day as if it's your first day, with no preconceived notions. On the third day of practice, I'll go out and figure out what I'm going to do." A lot of times, a pro like Howell finds himself figuring out the pattern for getting bites in the last few hours of practice.

In a sense then, there is no such thing as bad practice day. You've just spent two or three days eliminating water that is not productive for you, and your best strategy is to fish the water that you haven't already eliminated. Howell points out that repeating what already didn't work in practice is a plan for tournament disaster.

On Lake Wheeler in 1998 during an FLW event, he clearly remembers a less-than-satisfactory practice that turned itself around. It was also the tour event that earned him $100,000 and propelled his bass-fishing career. During this tour, Howell had five whole days of practice available to him. "I caught five bass in five days, and three of those bass were caught on one day! So I had three days where I didn't catch a fish." This was a critical event, primarily because he was on the short end of the financial strap. "We were really in debt and needing to make this event."

Howell continues, "I went out to this area that I wanted to fish and the wind was blowing big whitecaps across this flat. I couldn't fish it because it was so windy. But every time I went by there [during practice], I had a gut feeling that I needed to

be fishing out there." He never was able to pick up a fish in that flat during practice, but the next morning of the tournament, he had that gut feeling again that he should fish it. "So I went onto this flat, the wind wasn't blowing, and starting throwing a Rat-L-Trap. . . . Right off the bat, I caught a good fish, then a 5-pounder. Then I caught a few more."

Howell was focusing his attention on little patches of grass that he found in the flat, and he put together a good pattern for that location. The result was about 15-plus pounds of fish on the first day, and he was leading the event! "The second day I go out and start fishing around [the flat] and didn't get a bite. I started moving around and found another little patch of grass out in some stumps." In short order, another limit was on board his boat. With those two catches, he was able to make the top-ten cut.

By the time Howell got to the third day, the wind had kicked up again, making it impossible to fish that flat-water area. "I moved around [the lake] again and found another little patch of fish and caught another 9.5-pound limit." This allowed him to make the cut and fish against the likes of Rick Clunn, Tommy Biffle, and Larry Nixon. "It was all the big dogs and little old me that nobody knew."

On the last day of the tournament, conditions changed again and Howell could not catch fish where he had caught them the day before. He managed to catch four, and in the last minute and a half before he had to check in, he decided to make one last cast. That cast caught his fifth and last fish, and it weighed in at 2.5 pounds. "I checked in with twenty seconds to spare and no camera boat in sight to record that last fish. The only guy who saw me catch it was the check-in boat. I ended up beating Rick Clunn by one ounce." It just goes to show that it doesn't matter what or how you do in practice, it's what you do in the tournament that counts.

Swett: If he's not doing well during practice, Swett will sometimes employ the "bent rod" pattern. That's when he tries to learn what pattern is causing nearby anglers to get into fish, hence the "bent rod." "If I'm doing well during a practice, I'm not particularly concerned about other fishermen. But you always want to be aware of your environment. When you're on a tournament lake, other fishermen are part of that environment. You need to be aware of that. You don't bank on that, but you need to be aware of what's going on around you.

"Most of the guys out here on tour, they know the [seasonal] patterns. They know what's going on [in a body of water]. Generally, the person who wins the tournament has found something that is a little different that takes fish. We all have our seasonal patterns and our favorite baits to throw, but so do a hundred to two hundred other guys doing the very same thing and looking at the same water. They all have relatively the same information. Sometimes during practice, the very best school of fish can sort of get beat up a bit. They can get a lot of pressure and get hooked in the process." In this case, a slight adjustment may mean the difference between winning and losing. That adjustment could be as simple as varying the color, size, or speed of retrieve of your bait. It could mean changing the angle at which you cast and retrieve your bait in relation to where the fish are staging, or it could be a slight change in fish movement from one kind of structure to another.

Scalish: "A bad practice is not necessarily bad. A bad practice is telling you that whatever you're doing isn't working. So the next day you need to do exactly the opposite." Scalish suggests starting your "practice time" over during the tournament. "You start right where you left off and do things differently during the tournament. Some of the best tournaments you can have, you can also have the worst practice days in."

CHAPTER TWELVE

Developing Your Tournament Strategy

Developing the right tournament strategy is the key to increasing your chances for a win, or at least a check. Tournament strategy is a multifaceted plan that has several parts: 1) where you want to fish, 2) when you want to fish, 3) how you want to fish, and 4) what baits you want to fish with.

Ask successful tournament professionals what role strategy plays in their success, and they'll tell you it is a critical part of it. After days of practice, having a solid strategy for winning the tournament is the foundation for getting there. However, strategy has an Achilles heel: change.

What if the weather dramatically changes? What if the pattern you've developed in practice draws yawns from the bass during the first day of the tournament? What if your boat breaks down right in the middle of the tournament? The list of "what if" variables can go on and on.

You can have the most logical performance- and experience-based strategy, but any kind of variable can put a big kink in it. Then you have to do something that is rarely talked about in popular fishing magazines: You have to make decisions.

Sometimes a few, sometimes many, but you will have to make them.

Besides developing the ability to come up with a solid strategy for winning a tournament, you need to focus on becoming a highly effective decision-maker. There is no one right way to develop, execute, or readjust your tournament strategy. It's a personal journey that is shaped and sharpened by only one thing: experience.

Tournament Strategy Options

Jimmy Mason: Mason is big on being mentally organized as he puts his tournament strategy together. "Stuff becomes more real when I write it down. I organize myself so much better when I write it down. Each day during practice I'm making notes, and each night I'll organize my notes. The night before a tournament, I'll go through my notes and write out a fresh list of goals, which are the areas I want to fish during the day, in the order I plan to fish them. Basically, I like to make an outline of what I expect to be doing the next day. As I do this, I'm picturing the day unfolding [during the tournament]. At the

Jimmy Mason will make detailed notes regarding key areas he wants to prioritize and fish during his practice time. DAVID DIRKS

same time, I'm keeping an open mind and am ready for anything."

Writing out his strategy gives Mason a sense of confidence and lowers his anxiety level before the tournament. It seems to make sense. If you have a plan or outline of what you want to do, then you'll have at least a stronger start. Compare that to someone who does no planning before the tournament and just "wings it." You might expect that person's anxiety level to be just a bit higher.

Terry Scroggins: "If you go to one particular spot on your home body of water, you can't catch [fish] four days in a row off of it. So don't come out to a brand-new lake and try to do it. It won't work. Don't be afraid to fish new water. That's the number one key. If you look at all the big-name guys out here [on the tour] that do really well, you'll see that they don't stay in one spot. They cover a lot of water, and they are not afraid to move forward and see what's ahead of them. You can't get hung up on what happened yesterday. Keep moving and swing for the fence on the move.

"Ninety percent of the guys out here can look at a lake and say, 'That's where the fish should be.' And that's right. But when we come to an event that's a week long, with three days of practice and four days of tournament, those places get hammered. So what you've got to do is find some off-the-wall, key places that nobody is going to find. Those spots are not going to be as good as, say, a point, a super-ledge, or a

bridge piling, but over a four-day period, those places are going to get beat up. Then they become no good as spots. Catching one or two fish on a particular spot might not be considered very good, but those one or two fish will make a difference. These tournaments are won by ounces. Very seldom does someone get blown away by 3 or 4 pounds. Those two or three fish could make a very big difference."

Scroggins believes that if your strategy is not playing out during the tournament, the best thing to do is not worry about the last cast, just think about the one you're getting ready to make. "That happened to me this year. I lost two fish in the last thirty minutes of a tournament. I finished second but would have won it if I had caught either one of those fish. You can't get caught up in that. Stay focused on moving ahead."

Tournament fishing is not just about trying to win for money, it's also about accumulating points that you'll need to stay in the game. "When you come out here and fish the Elite Series, Open Series, or FLW Series, it's all points-related. Before a tournament starts, everybody has the mind-set to win it. They are trying to win the event, but sometimes that doesn't work. You can't always swing for a home run. If things are not working, you need a backup plan where you can go and catch a small limit [of fish] to keep those points up. That's important. When I go out to practice, I try to find big fish. I know and everybody knows that isn't going to happen every time. Along with finding those big fish, I try to find numbers of fish as well."

Scroggins stresses that the tournament-fishing business is like any other business and that it takes three to five years to get established. "You start learning these bodies of water. When you do find a spot, you mark it on your electronics and it's there for life." Over time you'll accumulate a number of spots on your electronics gear that will make your fishing more efficient and effective. But again, there's no replacing real time and experience on the water.

"I've been fishing BASS since 2001, and the older guys are saying, 'Man, the competition is getting so much greater now.' The reason why is the electronics [we have] today. That's what is making anglers so much better." Scroggins points out that it's much more challenging, if not impossible, for a newcomer to the tours to make it quickly. This is primarily due to the fact that many of the pros on the tour have five, ten, twenty, or more years in tournament fishing. "They've seen that lake fifty times more than you have. You're not going to go in there and beat them overnight."

Paul Elias: Elias recommends keeping your strategy as basic as possible. "Look at the time of the year. It's pretty much known what the fish are doing in each part of the year. My way of doing it is I would pick one area of the lake and concentrate on that area. I wouldn't spend a bunch of time trying to cover the whole lake. If you

go with a preconceived notation about how you're going to fish or what lure you're going to catch them on, you're trying to force-feed the fish something that's not really working. So I will go to the lake with about fifteen rods rigged up and try to get the fish to show me what they are doing."

Elias considers rising water his toughest tournament-fishing challenge. "Get to the bank," he advises. "I don't care if you have to go through twenty acres of flooded timber to get there, you better find some way to get to the bank." Failing that, he says, you probably won't do very well. He also tries to locate riprap and works to establish a pattern that will produce a bite, especially during cold, rising water situations. When a lake is 5 feet above normal, the two main places Elias concentrates on are the old shoreline and the new [existing] shoreline.

Frank Scalish: "Always go to your best fish first. I hear guys saying, 'They won't bite until the afternoon.' Maybe you didn't find them in practice until the afternoon. And what if someone beats you to those fish and they wind up catching the mother lode at 6:30 in the morning? You have to go to your best fish first, period." Scalish points out that if you don't get a bite on those best spots in the morning, you can always return to them in the afternoon. "It's about pattern fishing, not about spots, so you have to be open-minded in the tournament. You're going to go to your best fish first and play it by ear. If you run to spot A and somebody is on it, you go to spot B.

"What you have to keep an eye on is pattern changes during a tournament. You may get to your A spot where you caught them [in practice] on deepwater cranking. You go there and you only catch one [on cranking]. Maybe the fish are now suspended in the water column and they're not relating to the bottom anymore. So you have to put on a midrange crankbait or drop-shot them."

Scalish classifies fishing spots into three categories: A, B, and C. "An A spot does not mean a limit [of fish]. It's a spot where I can catch giant fish or at least bigger [fish] than what I've been catching. To me, size matters. A B spot has a decent grade of fish and maybe I'll catch a few numbers [of fish] there. A C+ spot is where I can get a few bites. They're keepers but it's nothing to write home about. . . . A limit spot is a spot where I know I can go in there and catch five. Usually, with the limit spots, they are not the first places I run to if I'm sure I can catch five fish anytime I go there." For a useful way to chart your spots, see appendix B.

Scalish says that the type of structure and cover you're fishing should dictate your bait choices. "The water color is going to dictate your color choices. Good rule of thumb: When you're throwing soft plastics, match the soft plastics to the color of the water. If the water looks kind of green, throw a green pumpkin or watermelon. If the water looks brown, throw a green pumpkin or something dark. The clearer the water, the more translucent the plastic. The dirtier the water, the more solid [in color] the soft plastic should be."

Making Decisions—The Real Key to Success

Ask any bass pro what role decision-making plays in tournament success, and their reply will sound a lot like Randy Howell's: "That's the hardest part of tournament fishing. That's the part that separates the winners from the losers and the guys who make a lot of money from the guys who make a little money [on the tour]."

For even more clarity on the subject of tournament decision-making, listen to what Elias says: "I really believe that the decision side of the game can make you feel like a king or jump up and bite you in the butt."

Effective decision-making (that is, doing the right things to put fish in the boat) is not a topic you'll find in many bass books or magazine articles. There's a mountain of fishing advice available that doesn't add up to much if you can't figure out the "when" part of the equation: When do you decide to "run and gun" for another spot? Do you "stay and play" in a spot that hasn't produced much in the past three hours of tournament time? When is it time to switch tactics?

You can read all you want about how to use certain baits, fish the seasonal patterns, and find structure, along with the proverbial "10 Ways to Fish Cover." At the end of the day, however, it's your ability to make the right decisions that will propel you to a win or, at the very least, a check.

Scalish: Decision-making during a tournament is a combination of art and science, with more art than science to it. "The more time you spend [fishing], the better your decision-making becomes. You can't be a tournament pro overnight." Scalish likens the process of becoming a successful tournament angler to learning how to become a great public speaker. "If you want to get really good at public speaking, you've got to figure out how many times the average guy speaks [publicly] in a year. Then go do that ten times more in a year. Then you've got ten years' experience in one year."

Scalish points out the difference between local tournament fishing and the professional level of bass fishing. Anglers who fish the same local lakes "fish five tournaments a year and they're all on the same lakes. They start to do well on those lakes after a while because those are the lakes they fish. So they sit there and say, 'I can do it. I can be a tournament pro.' But what they don't realize is that touring tournament pros are seeing twelve different lakes, twelve different times a year, and different lakes every year with two days of practice. There's a big difference. You have to have the ability in practice to really cover water and really understand what you're catching or [why] not."

Scalish offers the following advice on deciding whether to run and gun or stay and play: "The pattern is going to dictate how I'm going to fish. If I'm fishing crankbaits on secondary points, I'm running and gunning like crazy. If I'm fishing deepwater brush piles, I'm running and gunning because I have to cover as much [water] as I can. If I'm structure fishing channel ledges or deep breaks, I'm going to take more time on those spots because it's all about the angle of your cast and hitting the sweet spot. That's the whole key to structure fishing—the angle of your cast. A lot of guys pull up on a hump or a rock pile and they'll make a few casts and say, 'There's nothing here,' and they'll leave. You could pull up on that same place and turn the boat around and load the boat because the angle of the cast is different and it's the right angle. So you're going to take a little bit more time with that stuff."

Successful structure fishing requires that you pay attention and let the fish tell you how they want the bait. It can sometimes simply take a subtle change in the angle of the bait presentation to make a fish bite. In a tournament, this could mean the difference between coming home and coming home with a check. "If you're sitting around begging fish to bite, you are probably not going to catch them. If you're on the right pattern, doing the right thing, you are going to get bit. If you're not getting bit, it's time to go."

There are a couple other variables that Scalish likes to narrow down: "Am I doing

Jerkbaits, like these XCalibur Twitch baits, mimic mortally wounded baitfish. When the crankbaits aren't working, try a jerkbait instead. DAVID DIRKS

poorly by not making the top-ten cut? Am I doing poorly by not getting a check? Or do I need a big day to qualify for the Classic? Let's say I'm doing poorly and if I catch a couple of fish, I'm guaranteed ten grand. But if I blank, I won't get the ten grand. Then I'm going to fish conservatively to get the ten grand. Let's say I have a chance to make the top-twelve cut for television and if I don't catch them very well, I'm not going to fall out of the $10K spot. Then I'm going to press—I'm going to do what I know how to do to catch a bigger bite and hopefully creep up to the number ten

slot. If I have a chance to make the Classic, and I need to really make a comeback, I'm going to fish for big fish. If I flip a lizard, I catch a lot of 1- or 2-pound fish, but if I put a big jig on with a Super Spook, I know I'm only going to get four bites a day but they'll be 7-pound fish, then I'll take that chance."

At Florida's Lake Tohopekaliga (aka Lake Toho) in 2007, that's exactly what Scalish did. "I was guaranteed $10K, but I was catching 1- to 1.5-pound fish. I had a spot where I could get a limit of 1-pounders, and I was in seventeenth place. One-pounders were not going to put me in the top ten, and I'm not going to fall out of getting a check—I already made the check cut. So I went flipping for nothing but big fish. I ended up catching two little ones, and that was that. I went for the big bites knowing that I wasn't going to get a limit but if I caught one, it would equal most guys' 1-pound limit if I got one big bite. So I decided to go for broke. I had nothing to lose money-wise but everything to gain if I could make the television cut."

Mason: "When you fish a lake a lot,

you begin to form opinions about different areas. Lake Guntersville is one of my home lakes and when I'm not fishing tournaments, it's one of the lakes I spend a lot of time on. The area on Guntersville that Kevin VanDam won a tournament in during 2007 was such a huge community hole, I never fished it in practice. Very few local tournaments are ever won off of it because it's fished so heavily. It's just not one of the better areas to fish. On the map the area looks perfect, but it gets so much local pressure that I really underestimated

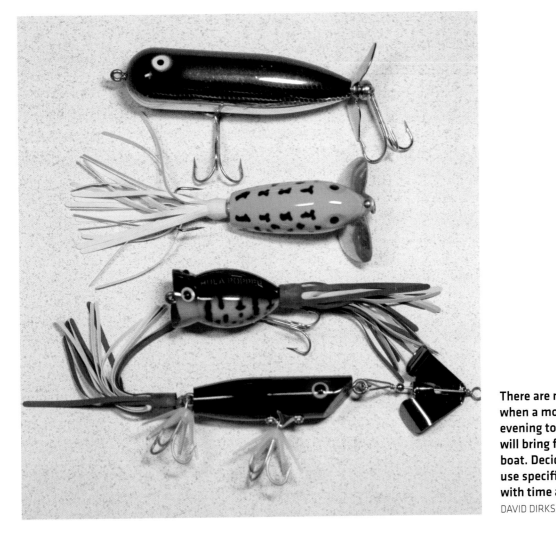

There are many times when a morning or evening topwater bite will bring fish into the boat. Deciding when to use specific baits comes with time and experience.
DAVID DIRKS

177

it. Because of my knowledge of the lake, I underestimated what would really be there, but that's where VanDam won the tournament." Lesson: Never overlook or underestimate the obvious.

Using a Lake Toho tournament in 2007 as an example, Mason illustrates the entire cycle from practice to tournament play: "Lake Toho was a very tough situation. September in Florida is always tough. Everybody knew it was going to be the lowest-catch tournament of the year. First day of practice, I had three bites; I caught two keepers. The second day I decided to spend my time on the lake two lakes down [from Toho]. I caught some small fish but never really found what I wanted until midday.

"Midday I went into a creek that fed into the lake. It had a really fast-flowing current. The water was about 10 degrees cooler, and it was falling really fast. In the first hour I had about fifteen bites. I knew I had found a great area, as tough as it was down there. Then I go and try to replicate that, as there were three other creeks on that lake. I went to all of them and I had a few bites, so I knew I had one good area and one fallback or secondary area to fish." He and his partner decided to go to the next lake down from Toho, Tiger Lake.

Fishing Tiger Lake, they found it had a great topwater bite. Tiger produced about ten bites in the last three hours of the day. Mason and his partner were both fishing topwater baits near the shoreline grass, and Mason noted that the fish they caught

during this time were quality fish: "I felt I had an area that I could pound hard and get some quality fish." The second day of practice went pretty much the same as the first day. "I was feeling a lot better after the second day. On the third day [of practice], I was back on Lake Toho again and tried to fish some areas I had fished in the past." He struggled during this last and final practice before the tournament began.

"That night, when I reviewed my practice, I found that the creek I had fished the first day [of practice] that had flowing water had the most concentrated number of bites. I knew it was going to be one of those tournaments where every fish counted. I also knew it was probably going to take about 8 pounds [of fish] a day to finish in fiftieth [place] and get $10,000." Mason's plan was to hit the creek first, knowing he could get a limit first thing in the morning on day one of the tournament. Next, his strategy was to go to Tiger Lake and work the topwater frog that had brought him several quality fish during practice. He was counting on the quality fish from Tiger to help him cull some of the smaller fish from his Lake Toho limit.

When the tournament began, Mason went into action, executing his plan. When he arrived at the creek, he found another angler already there—game over on that spot. "I spun around and headed straight to Tiger Lake. For whatever reason, the fishing there wasn't nearly as good as we encountered [during practice]. So I go in there and fish until about 10:30

a.m. I caught one, a 3-pounder. It was a good-quality fish for down there." Mason then wheeled around and went back to the creek he visited in the morning. He found out later that morning that the angler who was there before him had caught 10 pounds of fish.

His next move was to head back up to Lake Toho and start fishing the grass mats with a frog. In the next few hours, he caught seven keeper fish. After making some culls, he had a five-fish limit for the day with about 9 pounds of fish for the first day of the tournament. A top-fifty place was about 6 pounds of fish, so he knew he was ahead of his plan for cashing a check. The running and gunning he did on the first day, round-trip, was about 90 miles.

The second day of the tournament was about to begin and Mason needed to come up with a plan to keep his momentum going. The grass mat he had been fishing was only about 2 miles from the boat ramp. "I made a decision that I had never done at that level before. I went to the grass mat and never cranked it up until it was time to come in. I basically fished a 100-yard stretch back and forth for eight and a half hours. I ended up catching another 9 pounds, which put me in twenty-fourth place [on day two]."

Making the top-fifty cut allowed Mason to fish the third day of the tournament. "The next day, I gambled. I knew that there was not enough fish in the mat, or enough quality fish to make the top twelve

and get to fish the fourth day." So, on the third day, Mason ran back down to Tiger Lake and changed his technique. Instead of fishing topwater, he went to flipping a YUM Dinger, basically against the sparse vegetation. "Then I caught a 4-pounder, which is a good-quality fish. I did that for another three and a half hours and never had another bite. A little after noon, I ran back up to the mats and worked a frog fish and caught my limit." Needless to say, Mason ended up completing the Toho tournament in twenty-fifth place and took home a check.

There are a number of lessons here. Rather than continuing to run and gun to multiple spots, Mason ended up focusing on the fish-producing ability of one or two key areas. Long stretches between bites didn't deter him from fishing those areas for hours at a time until they produced the results he needed to win a check. He remained calm despite some practice-time setbacks and methodically fished the spots that he had a high degree of confidence in until they produced fish.

Howell: Howell looks at decision-making during a tournament this way: Either you make the right decisions, or you have to make your decisions right. "If you make a decision to run 50 miles upriver to flip trees, that's your decision, your commitment. If after three hours you've only caught one fish, your head starts playing mind games on you. Then you starting thinking, well, am I going to catch them or not? Do I need to keep doing this? Or do I throw this [pattern] out and do something else?"

If the decision is made to run 50 miles upriver and it's not working, Howell's strategy is to figure out how to make that decision work. "Even though it might not have been the right decision, I've got to make that decision right. I've got to figure out how to make that decision work for me. That's when you have to have confidence in your ability."

He emphasizes relying on your experience to tell you what has worked or not worked in this type of situation before. Once again, when it comes to fishing successfully, there is no substitute for time on the water and the experience it brings.

The amount of time available can also be an important factor in the decision-making process. In local tournaments, anglers only have about eight hours to make one or two key decisions about where to fish and how to fish it. That tight fishing time doesn't give you a lot of room to correct decisions that didn't work out.

"I've caught myself many times in a tough fishing day when my pattern is not working and my areas are not good. And then you think, well, I heard that so-and-so caught fish everywhere he went in 10-foot-deep water on a Carolina rig on points. Then I'll try that for an hour or two and not catch anything. Then your confidence is totally gone. You've lost everything you worked on during practice and now you're chasing somebody else's information that

usually is not accurate. I've learned to stay out of all that."

Elias: "I've had a lot of times when I've left an area, deciding the fish aren't going to do it, and I've got to go somewhere else. I've had friends of mine tell me I wasn't gone more than fifteen minutes and [the fish] turned on and everybody caught a limit. I ended up running and gunning and didn't have a very good day. I believe it's really an instinct thing. The guys that make those choices well are the guys that come out on top. You really have to determine how much weight it is going to take to win this tournament and the quality of fish in the area you are fishing. It's not hard to run off and leave an area where five fish are going to weigh 10 pounds. But it is hard to run off and leave an area knowing that if you catch five, they are going to weigh 20 pounds. So, you pull up and catch one 4- or 5-pounder right off the bat and then you go two hours without a bite. You start thinking: Do I need to get out of here and go finish a limit with that 5-pound kicker? Or do I stay and hope they turn on? Most of the time, I just stay."

But what if it's the last day of the tournament and you're behind? In this case, Elias takes a different track. From his point of view, if it takes 10 pounds a day to make a check and you're catching 5 pounds a day, in a two-day tournament, you're already 10 pounds behind. That tells you that you need a 20-pound day to get a check. Do you then stay focused on what you know you can do—that is, produce a

10-pound-plus stringer and maintain the points you can—or do you go for broke and try for the bigger fish, possibly zeroing out with a lot fewer points?

"I'm the kind of person that's going to change up and do something different and try to catch some big fish. If I zero, I zero. If I get one bite, I might get as much weight as I've been catching in the last two days. I'm going to go for the bigger sack."

Sam Swett's advice is to avoid going from "hero to zero." "If you look at [tournament] history, very seldom does a guy leading the tournament on the first day win the tournament. You have to make a decision on how to manage your fish. Hopefully your first five fish are good fish. If not, do you stay and cull up and take the chance of not catching anything tomorrow because you've caught basically the whole school of fish? Or you sore-lipped them all or spooked the school. That's when you see a guy go from 'hero to zero.' They'll come in with a 22- or 23-pound sack of fish. You'll hear them bragging, 'I caught twenty or thirty fish today.' Then they come in the next day and blank out, mainly because they caught them all the first day. They didn't conserve their fish."

A lot of it depends on the type of tournament you're fishing, says Swett. "If you're fishing a cumulative-weight tournament, where you take the weight you had into the 'top ten' day, or, like the FLW, where if you make it into the top ten, your previous weights are erased. Then everybody starts from ground zero." This requires you to calculate into your tournament strategy what you'll need to do in order to deal with both cumulative-weight and zeroed-weight tournaments.

Fishing with a Co-angler

Many tournaments, especially BASS and FLW tours, require a co-angler with you in the boat. There are two sides to this coin. One side is a great time for both the tournament angler and the co-angler, who coexist and make it work to their advantage. The other side of the coin is a negative experience, primarily for the co-angler. Reports of tournament anglers treating their co-anglers badly are not rumors—it happens. If you have to fish with a co-angler in your boat, the best strategy is to figure out how to make it work to your advantage.

Your co-angler can be a gauge for such things as color, size, and/or weight variances on baits. If they are outfishing you, ask yourself: What are they doing differently? Are they using a different size line weight? A 4-inch versus 6-inch bait? Try to modify your presentation to imitate what your co-angler is doing for success.

Elias: "My advice is to be as courteous as you can be to the guy in the back of the boat. At the same time, do all you can do to get your five fish in the boat first. That's what I've done before: get a good limit first and then ease up and let the guy catch some fish.

"I've had several times where my partner was throwing something different than what I was throwing and started catching fish. . . . I won a Super Bass tournament on Lake Okeechobee where I was flipping and got behind the first day. The second day I felt I needed to flip again just because of the potential of catching a big bag [of fish] and catching up. I saw a fish chasing a shad out in open water. I wasn't going to go out there and fish, but I changed my mind and made a short pass there. I was throwing a lipless crankbait." Elias was just about ready to leave that area when his partner caught a 2-pound fish. That was enough for Elias to revaluate his decision to leave the area for another spot. "I started throwing it out there, letting it go to the bottom and working it like a worm, and caught the heck out of fish and won the tournament."

Howell: "I found out over the years that it's best to treat people the way you want to be treated. A lot of pros won't even tell their partners what kind of tackle they have rigged. I hear so many bad stories from guys [amateurs] that fish with me. I tell my partner what I'm doing, how I'm fishing, and what kind of tackle I have rigged up, including baits, colors. He's going to be in the boat with me for eight hours, so I'm not going to lie to him."

Don't become a jerk. As someone once said, "Be nice to the people on your way up because they are the same people you meet on your way down." No truer words have ever been spoken. The worst thing a pro can do to an amateur is to blindside him and keep him in the dark. A pro with a

reputation for treating amateur boat partners badly soon learns that his reputation will leak and become known to everyone over time.

Howell makes it a point to let his co-angler know that he'll not only keep him informed on changes he makes, but also share baits with him as well. "Most of the [co-anglers] know that we're fishing for a living, so they are not going to push you too hard. They are going to fish and do their own things."

Howell wants his co-anglers to be successful. "If they catch fish behind, I take that as a positive thing." It's another competitive edge that can factor into a win and getting a tournament check. "As soon as someone catches one fish behind me, I try to figure out right away, 'Why did he catch that fish behind me?' That is especially true when the co-angler catches two fish in a row, fishing in the same area that you've just covered minutes ago. What kind of bait does your co-angler have on, and how is he fishing it?"

Using Your Electronics

While modern fish-finding electronics won't win you a tournament, they will help you to find and identify the structure that bass are relating to. To a tournament professional, the workhorse of their "tool set" is their electronics. The combination of sonar, GPS capability, and mapping software like Navionics is the best fusion of technology and tournament fishing. As

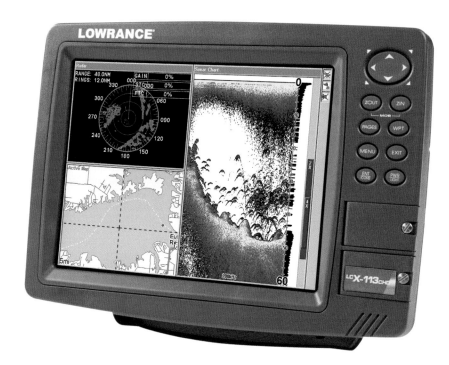

Good electronics with sonar and GPS combined is a must-have for any successful tournament angler today. NAVICO, INC.

they idle along a lake or river, tournament anglers have one eye glued to their screens and the other driving the boat.

It's a given then that if you want to compete successfully in tournaments, you need to have at least a basic electronics package on your boat. Some bass pros use a combination of hard-copy maps and their electronics, while others rely entirely on their electronics to mark key structure and fishing spots. The following tips will help you leverage your electronics for tournament success:

■ Make sure you know everything about your electronics package. You should know as much about how your sonar and GPS work as the manufacturer does, maybe even more.

■ Always check your electronics before you leave the dock. All that technology is useless if you can't put it to work during practice or tournament time.

■ Take advantage of all the data that today's modern fishing electronics packages provide you. Many models track basic weather patterns, including barometric pressure, which is a key variable in any tournament during any season.

■ Fishing electronics units that provide wide area coverage let you cover more area in less time. This is critical, especially during practice time, when you want to discover as many fish-holding spots as possible each day.

- Use your electronics to eliminate unproductive areas. Featureless areas of the lake bottom aren't generally productive, and your electronics can help you eliminate them from your list of potential areas to fish during the tournament.

- Units with 2D and 3D capability allow you to hold your boat position over underwater structure. Being able to see where your boat is in relation to the structure helps you determine how you will fish it: Do you need to back your boat off? Which side is optimal for your first approach?

- Use your electronics to follow along structure like contours, submerged creek beds, and drop-offs.

- Your electronics can help you locate schools of baitfish. Wherever there are baitfish, the bass can't be far behind.

- Higher-resolution screens help reduce the chances of false readings. Models with more pixels will help you distinguish between what is real and what's not. Don't skimp on power either. Most bass pros agree that a quality unit should have at least 3,000 watts of power. More power adds up to a faster reading of data (what it sees on the bottom of the lake or river) and greater accuracy.

- Marking every key fishing location is one thing, but using a marker or color that helps you identify or differentiate them later is critical for tournament fishing.

CHAPTER THIRTEEN

Favorite Tournament Tactics of the Pros

"Play to your strengths" is probably the soundest advice a tournament pro can heed in the midst of the competitive battle for the heaviest weight of fish. Survey any of the top twenty-five BASS or FLW touring pros, and you'll find a majority of the consistent winners stay on top because they play to their strengths whenever they can. They understand every aspect and nuance related to their tournament and check-winning tactics, and they continue to learn and gain more experience each year they

Terry Scroggins punches through thick vegetation searching for bass that other anglers will pass by.
LURENET.COM

fish. Yes, they also know how to exploit other fishing tactics, but they never forget what has brought them their success.

The season will certainly be a big influence and will determine what tactics you'll use in any tournament. That said, year after year our six pros use certain tactics in multiple seasons. Seasonal influence will only tell you where the fish are. Deciding which baits to use is generally based on how well you know how to use them to catch bass.

Terry Scroggins

"I'm from Florida, and that's where I learned how to fish. In Florida everything is shallow water [fishing]. Naturally, I'm better at fishing shallow water than water that is 30 or 40 feet deep. My number one technique is flipping grass cover, and that works all over the country. It's easy for me to come to a lake and ride around the lake and see grass floating on top of the water. It's visible. You don't have to search for it. As far as your electronics, you can go 50 miles an hour and cover a lake and see if there is any [grass] available. The downfall of that is that everybody else can see it.

"Take Lake Guntersville, for example. It's just full of grass. When I go there, that's what I look for. And I treat the grass mats just like I'm going down a creek. You want to fish all the points, the pockets, and the isolated mats. What I do is get the biggest weight available that I can get through the cover [grass]. I want to get my

bait in where someone else can't. Look for the things that everyone else is going to overlook, or they don't have the drive [it takes] to get in there.

"Let's say you have a big grass mat and everybody is fishing outside of it. On the inside of it, let's say the middle, there might be a little hole or a thicker matting of grass. You have to take the initiative and go in there and get to it. A lot of guys won't do that. They'll overlook it. You have to find things that everybody overlooks."

For punching through and working thick grass mats, Scroggins likes to use the YUM Big Show Craw, which was specifically designed for this purpose. Punching through grass allows him to find those bass that will react to his bait that's crashing through the thick mat. It's the reaction bite that gets him the fish he needs to win tournaments. In grass, Scroggins notes, "Tubes work really well."

When flipping heavy cover, you need dark colors: black/blue, black/neon, and brown/orange. "With thick grass, it's dark down there. It doesn't matter what the water clarity is, it's dark in that stuff." Scroggins goes on to say that "the number one mistake people make when flipping heavy cover when they get a fish is pull him out of there. You need to go in there and get him." He means reaching into the thick grass mat and grabbing the fish out. "Set the hook, get him hung up [in the grass], and go dig him out."

To find the right weight that will work in the grass mats he's fishing, Scroggins will

Scroggins specifically designed these YUM Big Show Craws to punch through thick grass mats. Bass hidden in those mats will strike viciously at baits that make it through. DAVID DIRKS

Scroggins recommends pulling fish out of thick vegetation by hand instead of using your rod and risk losing a quality fish. LURENET.COM

rig four flipping rods with four different weights—1½ ounces, ¾ ounce, ½ ounce, and ¼ ounce—and all tungsten sinkers. He then sets the reels up with 65-pound braided line and uses 5/0 hooks. "The reason I use four different weights is the rate of fall going in through the cover. You want a weight that will go through the cover freely and doesn't slow the bait down—you want it natural going through there."

If the grass is sparse and/or more broken up, he'll switch from braid to fluorocarbon lines. A good rule of thumb on what types of line to use on grass mats:

"Anything up to a ¾-ounce weight, I use fluorocarbon. Anything over, I use braid." He uses a 7½-foot flipping rod that's has a medium/heavy to heavy action.

Sight fishing during the spawn is another key technique that Scroggins will employ across multiple tournaments. If the tournament schedule allows it, you can find yourself fishing through the spring spawning period from February (for example, in Florida) all the way through June (in New York). During the spawn, Scroggins will sometimes use his "tomato stakes" technique on the last day of practice and in the

Scroggins lifts another hefty bass from the thick lily pads using a Texas-rigged YUM Craw Pappy. LURENET.COM

last few hours. Using a cut piece of wood about the size of a wooden stake used to hold tomato plants up, he will mark the spot where he saw the bedded fish with a stake (near the bed but not sticking in it). Marking a bed that has a fish on it enables Scroggins to throw to that fish without spooking it. "When you come back in the morning during low-light conditions, you can't see that bed but you can see the stake. I always say, if you can see the fish, the fish can see you. The bigger the fish, the harder they are. So what we like to do is take those tomato stakes and stick them right outside of the bed and mark the bed, then come back the next morning and make a cast to that stake. Nine times out of ten, you'll catch that fish."

For fishing spawning bass, Scroggins's go-to bait is a YUM Craw Pappy in green pumpkin. "If you can see the fish, the beds, the water clarity is good and green pumpkin in clear water is good anytime. For fish that aren't larger than 4 or 5 pounds, using a drop-shot is huge. It works really well."

Scroggins relies on his electronics for offshore structure fishing. When fishing deep water, he hones in on contour lines and fishing breaks.

He recommends covering a lot of water during a tournament, but that doesn't mean you fish fast. "Fish with patience," Scroggins says. He defines that as slowing down your presentation to the fish. "When you feel you have your bait in the strike zone, you need to really slow it down. A lot of your bigger fish are a lot slower to bite. If you're throwing a Carolina rig, Texas rig, or jig, a lot of times you let it sit there for a while. That makes a big difference. A lot of guys can't do that. It's hard to leave your bait sitting there. I've learned over the last four or five years from experience that when you need to, slow it down. I might fish fifty to a hundred spots a day. Instead of making a hundred casts in there, I'll make fifty, but they are quality casts. Let your bait soak up a bit more."

Randy Howell

Howell is partial to sight fishing for bass during the prespawn, spawn, and post-spawn. He equips himself with the right tools to make sight fishing highly effective. First, he makes sure he has the best pair of polarized sunglasses possible. "If you can't see them, you can't catch them," he says.

Knowing that some bass on the spawning beds can get skittish, he goes out of his way to keep some distance between himself and the bass. "I'll move out a little, make a big loop [with the boat], then circle back around and sit out and watch the fish return to the bed. I try to see exactly where the bed is and locate the exact spot the fish is sitting on. You can fish all around a bed and the fish will never get active to bite your bait until you get it right on that very small 'sweet spot.'" The "sweet spot" is about the size of a quarter and is where the bass has laid its eggs on the spawning bed. Bass will look to protect the sweet spot from other egg-eating fish.

"My bait of choice is a 4-inch pink Berkley Power Craw. It's bright and hot pink so that you can see it from far away. The fish are not keying on the color because they like hot pink. I'm keying on that color because I can see it and present the bait properly and see how the fish reacts to it. About 75 percent of the time I can catch them with that pink bait." Seeing the bait helps Howell avoid foul-hooking a bass during a tournament, which can cost you a fish that would normally count toward your total weight.

Howell prefers to fish that bait by making accurate casts right on or near the "sweet spot" and leaving the bait still. "I'll try to get [the bait] to where it's most protective. When the fish moves away, that's the time you can get your bait on that spot without scaring it. As soon as I see the fish look at the bait, seeing something on the bed eating its eggs, I'll start this really subtle shaking of the bait. I'm trying to make the bait quiver right on top of the eggs, like it's down there eating the eggs. That's when you'll see the reaction [from the fish] and know whether he's going to bite or not. If he swims up and looks like he's troubled by it—he starts to invert and stand on his nose or moves around a lot—you know you're really bothering that fish and he's getting nervous. Once you shake it enough, [the bait] will slide out of the spot."

If the bass relaxes once the bait is out of the "sweet spot," you should recast quickly. According to Howell, you don't want to give the fish time to relax. "You want to quickly keep him stirred up as fast as you can get the bait back there and shake it . . . keep bombarding that fish and make him attack [your bait].

"If the spawning bed is in an open area, make a cast past it, sometimes even casting your bait onto the shoreline. That allows you to drag the bait quietly into the water without making any splash and scaring the fish. If the bed is situated between two tree limbs, under a bush, or somewhere you can't drag up to it, that's when you have to make those real subtle pitches." This is where your casting ability comes into play and making accurate casts is key to success. "You want to have a real controlled, subtle pitch to take [the bait] down to the bed without making a big stir."

The ability to catch spawning bass on beds is critical to tournament success. It's not easy to catch bass on beds, it's just easier to locate them. Knowing when a fish is "catchable" is a crucial skill that Howell hones to a science during tournaments. "Usually, bass will make five circles around their [spawning] bed. If they stay away [from the bed], you may as well just move on. If they circle around with their circle getting a little tighter, every time they don't leave the bed as long as before, that is when you know you can lock down on that fish. Once it stops and sits still, then you know that fish is catchable."

If Howell finds that his efforts with the hot pink Berkley Power Craw are not meeting with success, he'll switch to

Make sure your baits are tuned and running well. DAVID DIRKS

a dark-colored lizard, like a 6-inch black Berkley Power Lizard. It may be that the darker bait looks more threatening to the fish or more like what the fish is used to seeing in the water. You need to keep in mind that when you switch to dark-colored baits when sight fishing on beds, you'll be a little more "blind" to what the bait is doing. A darker bait is just more difficult to pick out at almost any distance. That's why Howell will first use a bright bait pattern, like a hot pink craw, worm, or lizard.

"When I'm using [darker] baits," says Howell, "I'll back off the bed. Then you keep bombarding the fish with that black lizard, letting it do its job. A lot of times they'll bite it after you've moved away from the bed."

When fishing deeper beds or in very windy conditions, Howell will step up to a ⅜-ounce weight. A heavier weight allows the bait to sink faster and get into position on the bed quicker. "I've used weights as heavy as ½ ounce when I've had to. There is no rule on what the weight has to be. I'll rotate between the black lizard and a green pumpkin tube bait or a watermelon craw bait."

Another bait Howell will use on spawning beds is a large bluegill pattern, like a Mattlures Bluegill, which is a swim bait. For bedded fish that are 4 pounds or larger, using a large swim bait like a bluegill will often get them to strike when other baits can't. "It's real heavy, so I put it on a 50-pound-test Firewire Stealth braid line and put it on a big flipping stick."

Howell will swim the bluegill right up to the spawning bed. "It's weighted so that it'll sit on its nose and it looks like it's just standing up on the bed eating eggs. You can let it sit on that spot and start quivering that bluegill. It's a good big-fish bait, and it's also one of the baits I go to to get the really hard fish to bite."

One challenge that pros often have to face when fishing bedded fish is deciding when to give up and find other fish. Most pros will tell you that it's the confidence you have in your ability to find and catch fish that determines just how much time you'll spend trying to catch one big fish. It makes sense—the less confidence you have, the more time you'll be willing to spend on that one big fish you can see. The danger is in the eating up of valuable tournament fishing time. The time you use up on trying to catch one big fish on a bed is something you can't make up for. Highly confident and experienced anglers will spend less time on a big fish they can't entice to bite. They know when it's time for them to move on and find other fish.

Howell's next top presentation is shallow cranking, which he defines as crankbait fishing from the surface to 7 feet of water. "I have probably more shallow-water crankbaits in my boat than any other [lure], with about seven or eight boxes in my boat all the time.

"My number one shallow crankbait is a 0- to 5-foot runner." He uses a Bandit 100 Series shallow crankbait because it has a square lip instead of the standard round lip found on most crankbaits. Howell prefers the square-lipped bait because it ricochets better off of heavy cover like wood and stumps. "You want something that will bang off of cover and not hang up. If I see a lay-down tree with forty limbs on it, all the way out to the boat, I know that somewhere along there, there is a bass ready to eat. The worst thing to do is to throw the wrong-style crankbait into the right place. If you hang [the crankbait] up, you've ruined the whole place and you don't get the chance to get that first-reaction bite. A reaction strike on a crankbait in cover is usually the first cast. That's why that cast needs to be accurate, and the right bait that will bounce off [of cover] and get that strike."

Howell prefers crawfish baits in red and brown, in various shades from darker to lighter. "If you're fishing rocks, wood around rocks, or clay banks, you have to make an educated guess if the fish are feeding on crawfish or shad. I'll start with my confidence colors like a spring craw or one with pearl white with a chartreuse back that has some flash to it like a shad." He'll then let the fish dictate which colors to use based on his results.

His next favorite crankbait is one that rattles, like a Berkley Frenzy, especially during the spring and early summer months. Howell will move on to quieter crankbaits during the middle and late summer, when air temperatures are higher. He will use either lighter shad-imitation colors or a color like fire tiger. "Fire tiger is a

good all-around color to use when they're feeding on shad or crawfish." When water conditions are murky or clouded, the fire tiger color shows up very well and has a good flash to it.

"If I'm throwing balsa-type baits up into shallow water around fish that are in wood cover—with the water typically colored, stained, or even muddy—my favorite color is a yellow chartreuse with a black back and an orange belly. That gives [the bait] some flash."

Flipping and pitching give Howell the flexibility he needs to meet a wide variety of tournament conditions. He uses a ½-ounce Lunker Lure Rattleback jig. As for colors, he says, "You really don't have to get too fancy on your colors for a jig as long as you have a black/blue/purple type of color. You can fish that color [combination] almost anywhere you go. If I get into really clear water conditions, then I'll go to a more natural color like green pumpkin or watermelon/crawfish-type colors."

When presenting your jig when pitching or flipping, Howell suggests always putting your bait right where you think the fish is going to be on your first flip. "That's a big key. Lots of times people try to work their way up to the sweet spot and make a little noise and spook the fish. Most of the time on a big fallen tree or big bush in the water, the fish is going to be right in the center of it, right in the thickest and tightest part of the bush or tree. I'll put that jig right in there and let it fall down. Most of the time the bass will bite it on the fall. It's really critical to watch your line as it's falling. They'll have [the bait] in their mouth and you won't even know it." Once you break through the grass and you see your line just stop, or you pick up and feel that mushy tension on the line, setting the hook is your next move. Doing this immediately is critical to boating that fish.

"Hydrilla and milfoil mats are real thick, and usually a jig is not as good there. That's where I'll use a plastic bait with a big tungsten weight; 1 ounce, 1¼ ounces, and 1½ ounces are the three big weights for punching through matted grass." Howell

suggests pitching your bait high into the air and letting it come straight back down so that it plunks through the grass. This method is used by many pros on thick grass mats, hence the name "plunking."

Howell uses a 7-foot, 6-inch heavy-action flipping stick matched with a fast-retrieve reel filled with 65-pound braided line. He also advises using a sturdy, well-made hook when flipping soft plastics on thick grass, since it has to be able to stand up to the pressure of the rod, heavy line, and weights. "You need to use a heavy wire hook that is rated for a heavy braided line."

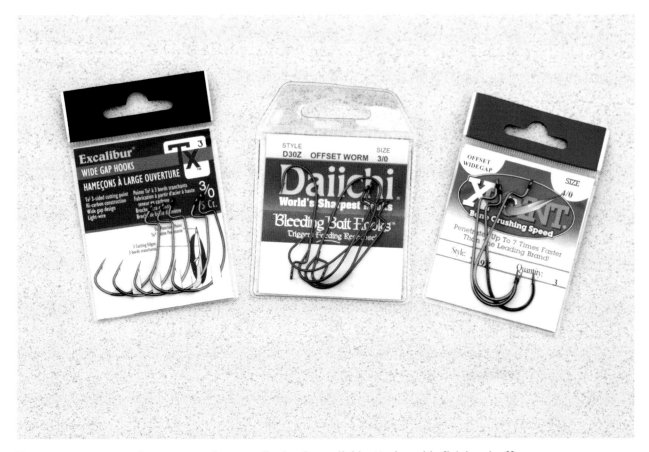

Tournament pros use the strongest, best-quality hooks available. Having a big fish break off because of a bad hook could mean thousands of lost dollars. DAVID DIRKS

It's important to note that Howell ties the braided line directly to his hook and uses a nail knot, which is used for heavy flipping and pitching. "Once I learned that knot, I quit losing fish," says Howell.

Frank Scalish

Deep-cranking summertime structure is one of Scalish's favorite tactics. "When you're looking at deep structure and you're idling over it with your [electronic] locator, there's always something different on a structural element. People get confused when a pro angler says 'structure' or 'cover.' They confuse the two. Structure is not cover. Cover is anything *on* that structure. For example, I find a creek channel and a good drop-off—that's the structure. If there are stumps on it or a rock pile, that's the cover. Anything on that structural element is cover.

"When you're structure fishing, you're looking for some irregularity or some form of cover on that structure. With deep-crankbaiting, it's not just about dropping a buoy on that cover and casting it out and bringing the crankbait back. It's not like that at all. You may have to fish 360 degrees around that structural element to figure out which angle the bass want. Bass definitely choose one angle or another. You're going to pivot 360 degrees around that structural element. The angle of your retrieve can mean success or failure for you. Once you make contact with the fish, you have to remember exactly how you cast [to

that fish]. That cast, over and over again, is what is going to catch fish for you."

As to why bass prefer a certain angle of retrieve over other angles, Scalish says, "There are a lot of reasons bass relate to structure and cover, most of which are current-generated. Bass relate to structure and cover in a way that gives them the optimal ambush point for feeding."

He recommends patience while you're looking for structure and cover to fish. "Make sure you're finding the cover on the structure. You may be literally 15 feet from a bag of fish, and if you're in a hurry and just start fishing it, you may miss that bag of fish and never know it." Structure fishing is extremely precise, says Scalish. "It's every bit as precise as flipping. People don't realize that because they don't see it. It's easy to fish what you can see."

Another thing that Scalish says to remember about deep-cranking is that there is such a thing as over-cranking. "Everybody thinks that if you crank it [the bait] superfast, it goes deeper. It's actually the opposite. If you retrieve superfast, it doesn't go as deep. So you want to have a retrieve ratio of about 18 or 19 inches per reel turn."

He also likes to crank the bottom. "I want my crankbait banging into things down there because as it bangs it deflects and turns sideways. It's not running or tracking in a straight line. The deflection of a crankbait triggers more strikes than anything except a pause. I've seen where I've hit an object, paused the crankbait, and the fish is just there. Pauses or deflections are huge [bite] triggering mechanisms."

Scalish describes himself as a "crankbait freak" who keeps his crankbaits simple. "I've got a shad pattern, which means gray back and pearl sides or black back with pearl sides—something that looks like a real shad. The Tennessee #7 shad is probably the best color for shad. Then I have a 'hot' shad pattern, meaning a blue back with a chartreuse belly or a blue-green back, prism-taped sides, and a chartreuse belly. So I have a real shad pattern and a 'hot' shad pattern. Then I go into a crawdad pattern. Crawdad does not necessarily mean it looks like a real crawdad. Basically, it's brown-bone-orange or brown-chartreuse-orange.

"The only variant I have in a color scheme is a perch pattern. I have a real perch pattern that I paint myself. It's a pretty accurate representation of a perch. Basically, I'm throwing that in all my northern smallmouth waters."

Scalish points out that you need to research what the predominant bait colors are for the water you are fishing. "If you're going down to Texas, you better have red with you. What's red? It's a crawdad pattern, and in that part of the world, they [crawdads] are red. You come up north and the crawdads are olive green.

"In dirty, dingy water I'll stick with primarily hot colors or white [as in black back, white belly]. It's a shad pattern, but white shows up [in the water]. Brown shows up in muddy water. Brown and orange is a good muddy water bait-color combination." Scalish has learned over time that experience helps you determine which color combinations are most effective on each body of water you fish.

Flipping is a very popular technique on almost any tournament trail, and it's one that Scalish excels at. "You're fishing visible cover, and it's total combat fishing. It's big lines, big rods, all muscle, and there's no grace except for the actual cast.

"Let's say you're flipping a stump. Did the fish come from the right side or the left side of the stump? Or the back of the stump or the front of the stump? Did he bite it on the way down or when you were jiggling it through the root system? These are things you've got to pay attention to because if he [took the bait] on the way down, it means he's suspending against the stump, in which case you don't want to throw a heavy lure. You want to throw something light that will fall slower, unless, of course, you generated a reaction bite, in which case you want something heavier because it'll rocket by him and he'll attack it. So you have to pay attention to how the bite is coming and where it's coming from: Was he on softwood or hardwood? Was it a willow tree or an oak tree? If you're fishing an area with nothing but flooded willows and every time you come to a piece of hardwood and catch one, why flip the willows?

"I once helped a buddy of mine practice for a local tournament. The lake was known as a flipping lake. It's mostly surrounded by flooded willow trees and willow tops. We ran out and started flipping because that was the bite for sure on the lake. We'd flip these willow bushes and catch little 12½- to 13-inch largemouth. I came up to a piece of hardwood and I flipped in there and caught a 4-pounder. I flipped on the other side of it and caught another one. So we set out to hit every piece of hardwood we could find. Sure enough, every piece of hardwood that we could find, we caught a monster off of it."

Scalish explains it this way: "It's like [fishing] a grass bed. Are they in the hydrilla? The milfoil? Or the eel grass? It's just their preference at the time, and that's what the pattern is. Most of the guys will see all the willows and go, 'I've got to flip the willows.' And they'll catch 1-pounders and be totally happy with that. They may flip 100 yards of willows and hit one hardwood and catch a big one. Then they'll say, 'I told you the willows have them!' My friend did nothing more than run the hardwoods, and he won it."

In terms of flipping baits, Scalish narrows it down to personal preference. "If you knock a fish on the head with it, he's going to bite it. My first choice of flipping baits is a lizard, mostly because hardly anyone throws it. It's sort of the forgotten bait. It's got a lot of movement. The tail moves, the legs move, it just creates a lot of movement. It helps to trigger the bite, so it's a good bait to use if someone rips through with a jig and I can go behind him with a lizard and maybe catch a few fish he

didn't get. My go-to colors for lizards are june bug, green pumpkin, and watermelon or red bug."

Scalish's next choice is a jig. "A jig is one of the number one big bass baits ever made. My color selection for jigs is even easier. It'll be black, blue, and purple or green pumpkin. . . . If I go through an area and get a few bites on a lizard, I'll usually go back through with a jig, just to see which one the preference is. Again, when I'm flipping in practice, I'm not hooking the fish." Scalish stresses that the idea with flipping is not to be snagging. "If you're throwing a jig and hanging up all the time, there are probably two problems: Either your weed guard is cut too short or it's too soft. Or the hook is too long or you're using the wrong head style."

Scalish uses a drop-shot as part of his tournament arsenal. "It's a fish-catching tool. I don't see how an angler in this day and age could leave for the water without having a drop-shot rigged. It accounts for so many fish and so many quality fish. You can deep-structure fish with it, you can sight fish with it, you can flip docks with it." His top choices for drop-shotting are 4- and 6-inch Houdini worms and YUM Dingers. He prefers 7- to 7½-foot medium-action spinning rods and thinks that most people tend to drop-shot on too soft of a rod.

"When I fish boat docks, I put the Houdini worm or YUM Dinger on a flipping stick and use 17- or 20-pound line. Same thing when I'm fishing grass. For

Weedless jigs, like these Booyah jigs, are specifically designed to punch through tough vegetation and provoke a reaction bite from bass. DAVID DIRKS

grass, I'll rig it on braided line and put a 1- to 1½-ounce sinker at the bottom of it to poke holes through the grass. It's not just a finesse technique—it has grown a lot of legs."

Scalish's favorite way to fish is the deepwater finesse style of drop-shotting. "It accounts for 90 percent of the smallmouth I catch and probably 60 percent of the spotted bass I catch. It's a tool. I'm using a 7- to 7½-foot Powell spinning rod with 10-pound-test fluorocarbon. I very rarely go lighter than 10-pound fluorocarbon when I'm drop-shotting because

fluorocarbon doesn't reflect light, so it's almost invisible to the fish." He recommends going to a lighter line only when you need to go to a lighter weight. Scalish encourages anglers to experiment with drop-shotting and to remember it's not just for light-line fishing: "You can wacky rig, Texas rig, and flip heavy grass with a drop-shot."

Scalish himself is always experimenting, such as with the length between his weight and the hook. "I have had situations where I've had the weight down and the hook 3 feet above it, and that's how I caught all my fish. When I lowered the hook closer to the sinker, I didn't get bit because the fish were suspending off the bottom. You want to pay attention to where those fish are in relation to the bottom.

"Make sure your line diameter doesn't exceed your weight's capacity. The whole key with drop-shotting is to be able to feel what it's doing down there [in the water]. If you use too light a sinker with too heavy a line, the line has a tendency to 'float.' It doesn't really float, but you can't feel anything. Therefore, you're not going to be as successful at it. A lot of the bites with drop-shotting are so subtle. Now, obviously, some of the hits are unbelievable, but most are very subtle and soft. If you're bed fishing with a drop-shot, you want the hook to be 3 to 6 inches above the weight.

"If you're fishing for spotted bass or smallmouth, get way above the weight. Largemouth can be 6 to 12 inches above the weight. When drop-shotting grass, what I do is stay in the middle of the pocket. For example, if you're fishing hydrilla, it's going to have huge caverns under the mat. So, you want to figure out where the bass are: Are they underneath the canopy? Or are they relating to the stalks, where it all converges together? That's going to dictate the distance from the weight to the hook."

Jimmy Mason

Flipping a grass lake rates high on Mason's list of tactics that contribute to his tournament success. "I like to approach grass mats looking for contours I would fish if there were no grass on the lake. The fish are going to be in the same structure places, such as creek channel swings, creek channel points, and main lake points. The grass is just the extra cover over the top of the structure. I'll put my trolling motor on a real slow pace and methodically make flips into the vegetation.

"What I'm really looking for in the mats are areas where it's slightly different. You'll see a different coloration of the mats, where you have an area of bright green grass and an area that has a brownish/blackish tint on the top. Those brownish/blackish areas of the grass mat are indicative of voids in the grass area itself. It's a real likely area to find fish in.

"You're also looking for areas with matted vegetation that's come to the top of the water and is starting to fold over onto itself. You want to make short flips with a heavy line like 65-pound braided line with a ¾- to 1¼-ounce tungsten weight and a small bait like a YUM Big Show Craw. It's a very compact bait that doesn't have any appendages that would catch the grass as it falls in. . . . Basically, you're looking for areas of concentrations of fish that are under the [grass] mats. On a grass lake, it's how you win or have high finishes."

When flipping, Mason puts a rubber bobber-stopper on his line before he puts his weight on. "That keeps my weight real close to my bait when I'm flipping in, so it keeps it from hanging up." A bobber-stopper is a small piece of rubber with a hole in it that you simply thread onto your line.

For grass flipping with braided line, Mason prefers to use a fairly soft flipping stick or a light-action flipping stick in a 7½ foot length. As for the reel, "You want to use a high-speed reel so that you can get the fish coming out of the cover." He cranks that reel at 28 inches per turn, so he has the ability to maneuver a fish out of the cover and boat it quickly.

During a tournament, Mason will have at least four rods rigged with flipping baits on his boat and ready to go. If he hooks a fish and boats it, he'll quickly put the fish in the live well, bait and all, and pick up another rod to immediately throw into the water. "This is a technique where the fish really group up tight in the [grass] mats. I want to get another bait back into the hole where I just caught a fish as fast as I can. If I get a bite on the next cast, that fish goes into the live well, hook and all. Then I grab the next rod. To me, it's quicker to have another rod ready to go. I save fifteen to twenty seconds by doing that, and that's critical. When I hit a group of fish, by having four rods ready, I can have four fish in the boat in less than

Jimmy Mason works a dock during a practice. Docks are consistent producers of fish, especially around release areas. LURENET.COM

a minute. It's really important when you hit that first fish, when they are grouped up, to get back in there immediately." Call it "speed fishing," but when every second counts during a tournament, it can make all the difference.

Shallow cranking is the arrow in the Mason quiver. He prefers to go with a square-lipped crankbait for shallow-water cranking because it deflects better off his targets. Square-lipped crankbaits move erratically from side to side as they travel in a straight line, and it's that erratic action that triggers the bites. Mason's main targets are creeks and rivers that have slightly stained water. "I'm looking for wood on flats, wood up the creek, channel bends, and where the flats transition into the channels." He also has his eye out for any cover on that structure like blowdowns, rocks, and especially docks that have fixed poles, not the kind that float.

Mason likes to set up his boat so that he's straight out to the target, whether it's a laydown or a dock, so that his crankbait is making contact as many times as possible. "When I'm cranking a dock, I want my crankbait to hit every pole on the dock. Same thing with the laydown—I want the crankbait to stay in contact with the branches and trunk of the laydown. A lot of your bites when you are shallow cranking are reaction bites. The vast majority of the bites you're going to get are right after your bait comes in contact with an object and deflects off of it." He has learned over time that stained water can make the fish

relate tighter to the structure. "It brings them up shallower and puts them on the targets a little better."

Like most pros, when it comes to color, Mason likes to keep it simple. "I pretty much throw two colors: One is a chartreuse root beer with a brown back, chartreuse sides, and an orange belly. The other is a Tennessee shad color, with a black back, white sides, and an orange belly. The only time I'll throw a different color is early in the spring—I'll mix in some reds just because a lot of the crawfish have a reddish tinge to them. I'll throw a goldish orange-red or even a red, but that's the only variation I have with my colors."

Mason uses 14- to 17-pound-test Silver Thread monofilament line. "I definitely use mono instead of fluorocarbon for this technique because the mono floats, so it helps to keep your bait from getting hung up quite as much." He prefers shallow crankbait rods that have a short handle, which allows for more accurate underhand casts, and uses a 6-foot, 9-inch Kistler graphite rod. He also likes 6:3:1-ratio reels that bring in about 29 inches of line per turn.

"Shallow cranking is a really aggressive technique. You're covering a lot of water, and you're aggressively throwing your crankbait at heavy cover. You're aggressively throwing it around high-percentage areas and basically looking for every target you can and making multiple casts. On a prime dock or laydown, I'll pull up my boat and sit there and make fifteen to

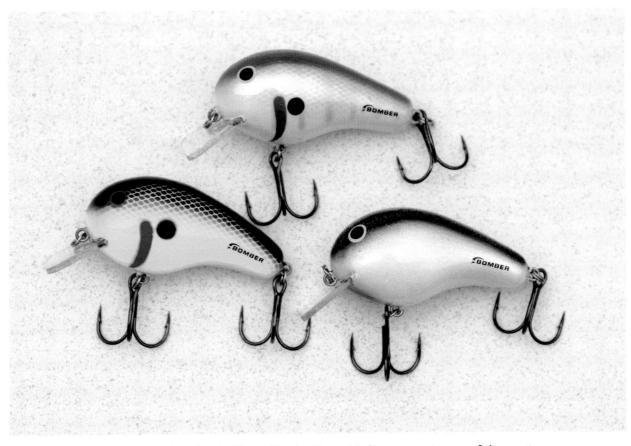

Most pros try to keep their colors simple. These Bomber B crankbaits represent some of the most popular colors on the pro tour. DAVID DIRKS

twenty casts." He points out that many anglers won't target heavy cover with shallow crankbaits because they are afraid to lose their lures. But in a tournament where the stakes are high, it's a technique that is designed to fill the live well for those willing to pursue it.

Bass will relate to cover in different ways depending on the time of day, Mason notes. "I'm thinking about Wheeler Lake, my home lake, where I'm practicing for the Bassmaster Open, and a lot of the fishing I'm doing is shallow cranking. The fish are definitely relating to different parts of the laydowns in the morning versus the

afternoon. The difference is that the TVA [Tennessee Valley Authority] is generating water starting around 12 noon."

Mason takes time to carefully position his boat so that he can make straight casts parallel to the sides of the dock and the pilings. This kind of boat maneuvering is critical to shallow cranking a dock in a tournament. "Until the fish tell me how they are positioned, I'm going to be keeping my angles for my bait as tight to the cover as possible."

He stresses the importance of catching the fish on your first cast. "Your first cast is your high-percentage cast. The fish is sitting there by the target and if you make a cast from a bad angle as you approach the dock, that fish is going to sense that bait. He's going to spin around and change his position and figure out what that bait is. If you wait until you're straight against the target, then you're going to ricochet it off of his face." That's when you'll get that first "reaction bite" that will get you that fish on the first cast. It's a subtle but critical point in tournament fishing. Get your boat into the best position to give you the opportunity to make a cast that is angled for maximum effectiveness. "To me, waiting to make the perfect cast at the right angle is super critical."

The shaky-head technique has taken both tournament and recreational angling by storm in recent years. It's also a tactic that rounds out Mason's competitive arsenal. "I always have two or three rods rigged for shaky-head in my boat. It's a 'check-getting' technique. I use a 4- or 6-inch YUM Houdini worm in green pumpkin—just about as simple as it gets. It's a really effective bait to fish in grass when it's heavily pressured or it's a post–cold front situation, when the fish are outside of the grass and really lethargic. You can fish the sparser grass with this technique. To me, it's most effective around rock and wood. I like to use as light a jighead as possible. The ⅛ ounce is the one I use the most, but if I'm fishing around riprap, I'll drop down to a ½₂ ounce where I can float my worm over the rocks to keep it from getting down into the cracks and getting hung up.

If I'm fishing deeper water, I'll go up to a ³⁄₁₆- or ¼-ounce weight.

"When we were at Clear Lake this year in the Elite Series event, thirteen of the fifteen fish I caught were on a shaky-head. I had a little over 62 pounds, and with the exception of two 4-pounders I caught on a swim bait, everything else came on a ¼-ounce shaky-head in about 25 feet of water, with a 6-inch Houdini worm. I was fishing staging fish, fish that were moving up on the spawning areas. The fish were pretty spooky, but they were also really grouped up. That ¼-ounce head would get down there really fast."

Mason also likes to use as light a line as possible when fishing open water. "I never go over 10-pound test, even when I'm skipping under docks. I use 6-pound test more than any other pound test. I always fish a shaky-head on spinning tackle. I use a 6½-foot Kistler medium/heavy spinning rod. It's a parabolic rod, so that it has an even bend from the midsection to the tip. I always use fluorocarbon with this method. I use 6-pound test probably 75 percent of the time, 8-pound test about 20 percent of the time, and 10-pound test about 5 percent of the time.

"A lot of times when you're casting a shaky-head, you want your bait to fall vertically, whether it's a pier pole, barge tie-up, retaining wall, or bridge pier. By keeping your bail open on the reel, it allows the bait to fall and not pendulum back towards you like you were using a baitcaster. Most of the spinning reel drags are a little better than a lot of baitcasters. So the spinning reel allows you to handle the light line much better."

Mason says that when things get tough at the end of the day and you can't get a bite on anything else, pick up a shaky-head and hit as many docks and pieces of wood on flat, rocky points as you can. "A lot of guys on the second or third day of the tournament will fish outside the off-limits area trying to catch release fish. This is a great way to catch release fish because it's a subtle and great finesse technique."

Sam Swett

Swett is another fan of the shaky-head technique, and he considers it absolutely indispensable for the tournament angler. "Power fishing is starting to go away. The big crankbaiters and Bubba baits are giving way to finesse fishing." He stresses that the increasing popularity of bass fishing and the larger number of tournaments being held on lakes increase the need for more delicate fishing presentations, like the shaky-head technique. It's not uncommon for a lake to have a two- or three-hundred-

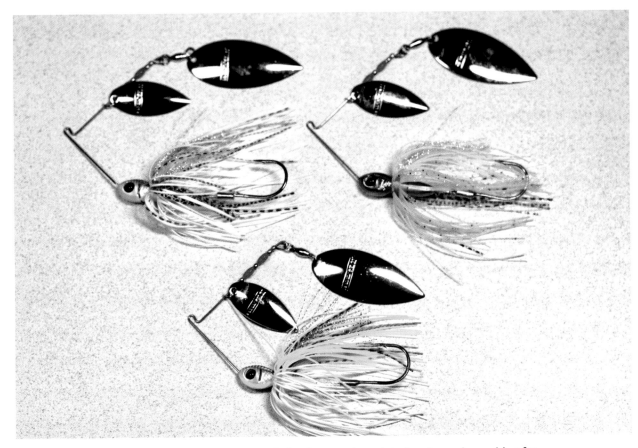

Spinnerbaits remain the tournament pros' top choice for covering a lot of water and searching for bass. DAVID DIRKS

Having a good supply of soft baits is critical for finesse fishing. DAVID DIRKS

boat tournament week after week during the season. "These fish have seen everything. The very small, finesse-type baits are what will catch fish. I use an All Star 6½- or 7-foot medium-action rod. Faster-taper rods allow you to impart that 'shakyhead' action to the lure effectively."

Swett believes that one of the best things a tournament angler can do is become one of the best casters in the world. "With the lake pressure and the popularity of fishing, pinpoint casting is very, very crucial in this sport. You want to get your baits to where other anglers possibly can't get to. You have to learn how to skip, pitch, and flip baits deep under docks or into heavy cover.

In general, Swett says, "A spinnerbait is a bait that can be fished year-round. It's a locator bait that helps me to find fish. It's a bait that can cover a lot of water and maximize your time if you're not on to anything."

Paul Elias

Throwing deep-diving crankbaits is Elias's "go-to" tactic. "I love to fish water between 8 and 12 feet deep that is close to deeper water. I like a diving bait because I can cover a lot of ground. It's a reaction bait that causes the fish to strike a lot of times. The potential to catch a big stringer is a lot better with a pretty good-sized bait in an area where you're going to run into schools of fish. That's what I'm constantly looking for."

Elias's number one bait choice is a Mann's 20+. "The reason is that bait has a wide lip on it and it goes through cover a lot better than most deep-diving crankbaits. It's a confidence factor because I've caught so many big stringers on it that I know its potential. That's what I'll start with." If that's not working, he'll switch to a deep-diving bait that has a narrow lip and a little wobble that causes the fish to strike. Typically, he'll have at least three different deep-diving crankbaits tied on rods.

Deep-diving crankbaits need to dig into the bottom in order to be effective, says Elias. He is looking for something different on the bottom of the lake—some kind of cover that the bass will use as their "house." "Most of the time I try to make as long a cast as I can, trying to cover more ground and get the bait down. When I feel that bait start to hit something or start to come over something [on the bottom], that to me is a potential place to catch a fish. I start paying closer attention. I hesitate the bait and try to get it to ride over and then speed [the retrieve] up. To me, that's trying to make something that's not real look alive. So I pay real close attention to what that bait is doing on the bottom." When he hooks a fish, Elias also pays close attention to the angle at which the fish took the bait. His next cast is lined up so that it's an exact repeat of the last cast, so casting accuracy is critical.

Again, the angle of presentation can drive your tournament performance. "If you throw 10 feet to the left of a stump or 5

Paul Elias tunes one of his favorite deep crankbaits. By adjusting the lip on the crankbait, he can change its action in the water. DAVID DIRKS

feet to the right of the stump, a lot of times you're not going to get a bite. There's an angle they want that bait to come through, and you can hit that stump from one direction five times and not get a bite. Then you can go around from a different direction and catch one almost every cast. You have to figure those things out.

"There are times when you are going to catch fish suspended on a crankbait or standing trees. If you're fishing the tops of trees, that's just like fishing the bottom— you want that bait digging into the tops of those trees. You want that bait hitting structure all the time, or hitting the cover all the time."

Boat positioning, especially when deep-cranking, is critical in order to get the bait deep enough. "If your cast is 50 yards, you want to have your boat at the most 20 yards from the piece of cover you're trying to hit. It takes that [additional] 30 yards just to get the bait down to that depth in order to come through that cover. A lot of people don't realize that. They'll see a hump and mark it and make a long cast to it. They'll think that crankbait is going to get down there and hit that hump." Of course, they miss the hump by a mile and miss fish that could help them win the tournament.

Elias is well-known for his "kneel and reel," a technique that he perfected and is now used by many tournament anglers. "I'm known for that just because I won the Classic doing that. I found a place on

Elias demonstrates his now-famous "kneel and reel" technique of getting his crankbait to run deeper. DAVID DIRKS

the Alabama River that was one of those instinct things that told me there should be fish here. I fished that place three different times before I got a bite on it. I caught a little 12-inch fish. This was during the pre-fish for the Classic. The last day I was there, I hit it one more time." Using a deep-diving crankbait, Elias caught 4- and 5-pound fish on back-to-back casts. Keep in mind that the pre-fish was in September and the tournament was being held in October. Cool weather during the tournament caused the bass to fall back into deeper water; however, some good-sized spotted bass came in shallower and took their place. "In order to get the bait down to where the fish had moved in to about 12 feet of water, I had to make as long a cast as I could. Then I'd stick my rod down into the water up to the reel and get the bait to touch that cover in 12 feet of water." And so the "kneel and reel" technique was born.

He uses a 7-foot, 11-inch rod that has a medium action and likes the longer rod because it allows him to kneel and reel. "I don't like a real wimpy rod. I like one that has some backbone to it with a flexible tip so I can load it up and make a long cast with it." As for reels, Elias prefers a 5:1 gear ratio. "There are times when you want to burn a crankbait, and there are times you want to take it really slow. Normally, a medium retrieve is pretty good with a 5:1 reel. The majority of the time I'm throwing 10- to 12-pound test."

Elias's favorite colors for crankbaits are simple but highly effective. He particularly likes the bluegill color, which is a brown or black back with chartreuse and an orange belly; the crawfish color, which is a black or brown back with an orange belly; and two shad colors: a blue back with chrome and a basic Gray Ghost pattern with a gray back, pearl sides, and a light orange belly. He believes that most bait colors are designed to catch fishermen, not fish, "so when you go into a store and you start looking at all these colors with such a wide variety, to me it's better to buy four of one color that you like instead of buying one of four different colors. You're going to lose crankbaits. If you're not, you aren't throwing them in the right place."

What would Elias use if he needed bait with sheer fish-catching power? "It would be a ⅝- or ¾-ounce lipless crankbait. On grass lakes, I'll throw it on braid and rip it through the grass. I'll use a 7:1-gear-ratio reel and rip the bait through the grass, trying to get reaction strikes out of it."

He also likes to work a lipless crankbait through flooded bushes with braided line. He'll fish it like a worm by pulling the bait along, letting it settle on the bottom, and then pulling it along again. He says it's not something you can do in heavy wood cover, but for lakes with grass and bushes, it's ideal. "It's probably the most versatile bait out there. You can throw it at shoreline cover, out in the middle of the lake, or in grass; you can flip it, pitch it, and swim it. It's just a 'go-to' bait that you've got to have."

Lipless crankbaits, like these Cordell Super Spots, represent some of the most popular color combinations. DAVID DIRKS

Elias says there is seldom a tournament where you're not tying on a jig at some point and throwing it. "I'm pretty flexible on the colors. I use jigs that are black and blue and green pumpkin. Most of the time I'll throw a ½-ounce jig."

He'll fish a traditional jig the same way he fishes a plastic worm. "I'll throw it out there and let it go to the bottom and work it back to the boat, picking it up and letting it fall. I'll swim it through grass. I'll swim it by bushes and docks. In deep water, I'll rip it off the bottom really quick, just by turning the reel handle fast and then letting it swim back down to the bottom. On certain lakes like Kentucky Lake or Toledo Bend, there are times when the bass want that jig ripped up off the bottom with your rod."

CHAPTER FOURTEEN

The Business of Tournaments

The thing that prevents most anglers from getting access to BASS or FLW tournaments is the cost. Entry fees are in the thousands. Then you need equipment, and lots of it. Many pros bring anywhere from twenty-five to forty rods with them to each tournament. And don't forget the bass boat, which with even a basic engine and electronics package is going to set you back $25,000 to $35,000. On top of all that, you can throw in the extra travel costs like gas, hotel, and food, in addition to those "emergency" repairs that show up at the wrong time.

The cost of operating on an eleven-or-more-tournament trail can run over $100,000 per year. Unless you have a dream job that allows you unlimited time off with a fat salary, it's a real reach without help. That's where sponsors come into play. Getting sponsors is not easy but not necessarily impossible either. It takes good, old-fashioned hard work and staying power to get and keep sponsors. But don't take my word for it—listen to what the professionals have to say.

Scott Rauber, a leading marketing consultant who specializes in helping anglers develop strategies for acquiring and keeping sponsors, knows just how tough it is to get them. "You've got to leave the fishing industry and look outside it for sponsors. The fishing industry as a whole is hammered for sponsors." He notes that the fishing industry is asked not only to sponsor tournament anglers, but also provide goods and services to an endless line of community groups, fishing clubs, and local and regional tournaments. "Look for someone outside the industry for sponsorship," he advises.

Rauber strongly recommends that anglers prepare a game plan outlining how they can help a potential sponsor land more business. It's not enough to say, "Slap your logo on my shirt and truck." You have to aggressively put together a game plan to actually help them attract business and new customers.

Network, network, network, Rauber advises. "Talk to as many people as you can to attract sponsorship. Don't leave anyone out. You never know who's going to be your next sponsor. Your most unlikely candidate might just become your full boat sponsor."

Part of being a pro tournament angler is helping sponsors sell more tackle. Jimmy Mason works with a customer during a tackle trade show. LURENET.COM

Your fishing success is not as important as everybody makes it out to be. Placing in the top five or ten in local tournaments doesn't earn you the right to get a sponsor. Businesses don't care who you beat and how many times you beat them, says Rauber. What they care about is whether or not you can help them sell more product.

The business side of tournament fishing is marketing and media, says bass pro Frank Scalish. Your tournament performances only enhance your potential media coverage. You need to have some marketing savvy in order to make it in the big leagues of BASS or FLW tournaments, and you have to be very comfortable and articulate when you are dealing with the media. "There are a lot of guys who can get media coverage because they can catch fish. But as soon as the media lights are turned on or a microphone is shoved in their face, they're at a loss," says Scalish.

"If you think you're going to get a sponsor because you tell him that you can fish well, you have another thing coming," Scalish points out. "Everyone in the free world who wants a sponsor, that's the first thing out of their mouth." A sponsor is

Frank Scalish signs an autograph while working a trade show. LURENET.COM

going to ask you how many boats or how many rods you've sold.

You will also need the skill of being able to deal with a wide variety of personalities. You'll have to learn to deal with abrasive people with a smiling attitude. Whenever you're on the road representing your sponsor, your sponsor's reputation always comes first. Run into someone who rubs you the wrong way while on a sponsor trip or show? Smile and make the best of it. If you handle the situation badly, it reflects on your sponsor. "No matter how crappy your day is or how bad you

feel at the time," explains Scalish, "you need to be in your 'A' game when it comes to your sponsors."

Terry Scroggins dedicates about 250 days a year to tournament fishing and helping his sponsors. He believes you need to make sure you are always adding value to your sponsor relationships, and that starts by making yourself available to them whenever they need you. "I tell my sponsors that I'll give them 365 days. If you need me, call me and I'll be there unless I'm already booked somewhere else," say Scroggins. He feels that it is a

Terry Scroggins works a tackle trade show as part of his sponsor responsibilities. He spends 250 days a year on the road, many of them at shows like this. LURENET.COM

major mistake for an angler to try to limit the number of days available for a sponsor. "If you want to get paid, you've got to work. They are not going to send you money to stay at home. Your job is to promote their product," he adds.

Almost every pro puts a quarterly or annual report together that demonstrates their value to their sponsors. This report includes how many events they attended that promoted their sponsors and how many advertising "impressions" were made during the course of the quarter or year. If you get sponsors at any level of tournament play, whether local or national, you need to show them the number of times you've directly or indirectly helped their business.

It's also critical to stay in regular contact with your sponsors. Scroggins says that the biggest mistake a tournament angler can make is to get sponsorship funding and then not stay in regular contact with them. Don't take your sponsorship for granted and put it on automatic pilot.

Finally, don't overlook the smaller businesses in your area as potential sponsors. The combined contributions of smaller local businesses can add up to a considerable amount of support for tournament fees and other related expenses.

Bass Pro Biographies

Tournament fishing is physically demanding. Maintain a good workout routine while preparing for tournaments. DAVID DIRKS

Paul Elias

Hometown: Laurel, Mississippi
Bassmaster Classic titles: 1
Times in the Bassmaster Classic: 14
Total (BASS and FLW) entries: 363
Combined career winnings: $1.32 million
Web site: www.indepthfishinglessons.com

Elias recalls that in his early teens, he seemed to have a knack for catching fish. "I always loved to fish. Every time I went with my friends, it always seemed like I caught more fish and bigger fish. So everybody kind of looked up to me and wanted to go fishing with me. I was very poor coming up in life. I didn't have a boat, so I had to rely on other people for a boat."

After finishing college, Elias took a job offshore and worked until he had enough saved for his first bass boat. After convincing his first sponsor to help him with expenses, he signed up for the American Bass Fisherman (ABF) tour. In his first two years, Elias placed well, finishing in the top ten. Eventually, he found his way to the Bassmaster tour and kept going from there.

Paul Elias
LURENET.COM

Randy Howell
LURENET.COM

Randy Howell

Hometown: Springville, Alabama
Times in the Bassmaster Classic: 9
Total (BASS and FLW) entries: 246
Times in the money: 90
Combined career winnings: $1,128,033
Web site: www.randyhowell.com

While many tournament pros got their starts as young recreational anglers, Howell took a different track. "My mom and dad bought a small fishing marina when I was eleven years old on Lake Gaston on the North Carolina–Virginia border." While devoting most of his time to fishing, Howell also worked the marina tackle store and the boat rental business at the same time. "I started guiding when I was twelve years old. I was actually getting paid for taking guys out on fishing trips."

Now, years later, he still gets plenty of mail and e-mail from folks that he guided as a young teenager. "My dad was a tournament fisherman and wanted to be a bass pro himself." His father, recognizing the natural fishing talent his son possessed, did everything he could to provide Randy with the opportunities to fish tournaments. "I fished local tournaments as a teenager and then fished the Redman tournament trail at the age of sixteen." At the time, Howell was the youngest to qualify for the Redman regional tournament. "I just never thought about doing anything else. I had no other plan of attack other than being a professional fisherman."

Jimmy Mason

Hometown: Rogersville, Alabama
Total (BASS and FLW) entries: 115
Times in the money: 38
Combined career winnings: $64,737
Web site: www.jimmymasonbasspro.com

Growing up about a mile from bass-filled Wheeler Lake in Alabama gave Mason the place he needed to learn the craft of bass fishing. His father, a local tournament fisherman, gave Jimmy his introduction to tournament fishing for bass. "I grew up fishing. I learned to walk during a family fishing/camping trip. I'd see Daddy come home after a tournament and talk about what he had won. So that's what I wanted to do. I wanted to be like Dad. As I got older, I'd fish with him and got the taste of tournaments by fishing team tournaments with him. I just got bit by the bug."

Jimmy Mason
LURENET.COM

Frank Scalish

Frank Scalish

Hometown: Cleveland Heights, Ohio
Times in the Bassmaster Classic: 2
Total (BASS and FLW) entries: 91
Times in the money: 33
Combined career winnings: $255,457

Scalish was about fourteen years old when he decided that competing in bass tournaments was something he just had to do. "I told my father that tournament fishing was what I wanted to do for a living. Of course, he laughed. Back then, it wasn't a living. It was glorified club tournament fishing." He fished his first bass tournament at age sixteen and took second place. Soon he was entering local tournaments throughout Ohio and gaining valuable tournament experience.

After getting a degree in marketing from Ohio State, Scalish established himself in advertising but the tournament bug persisted. "I started my own ad agency just so I could take time off to fish whenever I wanted to. And it wasn't just for bass. I fish for everything that swims." After his dad passed away in 2001, he decided to enter the pro tour by competing in a qualifier. "And I never turned back since. I qualified in 2001, and 2002 was my first full year as a pro and I won rookie of the year."

Terry Scroggins

Hometown: Palatka, Florida
Times in the Bassmaster Classic: 8
Total BASS entries: 126
Times in the money: 87
Career BASS winnings: $1,326,098

"I've been in a boat since I was two years old," says Scroggins. "I used to go out with my dad. I've been fishing my whole life. I started fishing bass tournaments with my dad when I was twelve or thirteen years old. When I turned sixteen, I started fishing tournaments on my own with other guys. There always had to be someone eighteen years old or older in the boat in order to meet the requirements."

In his second BASS tournament, Scroggins won handily and started his career by winning $50,000. Now, ranked one of the top twenty-five bass tournament anglers in the world, he's looking forward to many more years of competitive bass fishing.

Terry Scroggins
DAVID DIRKS

Sam Swett
COURTESY SAM SWETT

Sam Swett

Home: Covington, Louisiana
Times in the money: 26
Combined career winnings: $230,499

"I started fishing when I was too young to remember," recalls Swett. "I remember the very first bass I caught. We had a farm and a three-acre pond. I was seven years old and was using a Zebco 202. Ever since then, I was caught into fishing." In 1981, as a high school graduation present, his parents gave him a guided bass-fishing trip on Toledo Bend. Little did Swett know at the time that the guide they hired was with the legendary Jack Hanes, who was the second Bassmaster Classic winner in the very early days of BASS under Ray Scott. "He got me hooked into the tournament aspect of fishing."

A few years later, in 1988, with encouragement from Hanes, Swett entered his first bass tournament as an amateur. With that, he started beating some of the pros on the tour. Hanes pointed out the obvious to Swett: If you can beat some of the best pros in these tournaments, you could do well as a pro yourself. His continued success led Swett to pick up significant sponsors and go full-time on the tournament trail.

Helpful Tournament Forms

This form is designed to help you organize your practice time and keep track of the key spots you need to find before the tournament begins.

Category Spots	Practice Day 1	Practice Day 2	Practice Day 3
Category A Spots			
Category B Spots			
Category C+ Spots			
Limit-Out Spots			
Notes			

This form is designed to help you constantly monitor and improve your skill levels as a professional tour angler. Learning is a constant requirement for a successful tournament pro.

Top Strengths	Mid-Strengths	Weaknesses	Plan for Enhancement/Improvement
Your best presentations/ tactics where you have *exceptional* ability, skill, and confidence. These are your "go-to" tactics. Keep learning how to do them even better!	Secondary strengths with moderate level of ability, skill, and confidence.	Low confidence areas with low skill level and little expertise. Be honest with yourself—even the best pros admit their weaknesses.	How can you develop or enhance the skill levels of your strengths, mid-strengths, and weaknesses? What can you do during the off-season to build strength in all areas?

About the Authors

Karen Savik, born and raised in Minnesota, bought her first boat in 1991 and began tournament bass fishing in 1994. She turned pro in 1996 and fished the entire Minnesota-based Silverado Pro-Am circuit that year. Savik made history with her first tournament victory, which occurred in difficult downpour conditions at the Minneapolis Aquatennial Bass Championship in July 1997. With the win she became the first woman in Minnesota to win a professional bass tournament. She told *Outdoor News* at the time, "I was fishing against the best and never thought I would come in with a bigger bag of fish than them!"

Since then, Savik has focused on the national bass tournament trails, and for most of this decade, she has fished the FLW bass tour. In 2001 she became the first woman to qualify for the Everstart series national championship and finished the year in fifteenth place overall. Savik has remained competitive ever since, and she completed this book while on the road fishing the FLW tour during spring 2007.

In addition to being a pro angler for half the year and running a part-time bass fishing guide service on Minnesota's

Karen Savik COURTESY OF MITCH KEZAR, WINDIGOIMAGES.COM

world-famous Lake Minnetonka, Savik owns and operates a restaurant with her husband of twenty-seven years, Ken, in Wayzata, Minnesota. The Saviks live in St. Louis Park, Minnesota, and have two daughters, Britta and Kirsten.

David Dirks COURTESY DAVID DIRKS

David Dirks is a freelance outdoor writer. He writes a weekly outdoor column for the *Times Herald-Record* in New York State and has written for several outdoor magazines, including *American Angler*, *New York Game & Fish*, and *Boating on the Hudson*. He is a member of the New York State Outdoor Writers Association and the Metropolitan Outdoor Writers Association. He is also the host of the DirksOutdoors Radio show on WTBQ.com. He lives in Orange County, New York, with his wife, Christine, and four growing children.